THE ROAD TO RESTORING THE FAMILY

THE
ROAD
TO RESTORING
THE FAMILY:

LEAVING AN INHERITANCE TO OUR CHILDREN'S CHILDREN

Discover Forgotten Foundations

SENATOR MIKE MORRELL (RET)

XULON ELITE

Xulon Press Elite
2301 Lucien Way #415
Maitland, FL 32751
407.339.4217
www.xulonpress.com

All Scripture quotations, unless otherwise indicated, are taken from the Holy Bible, New International Version®, NIV®. Copyright ©1973, 1978, 1984, 2011 by Biblica, Inc.™ Used by permission of Zondervan. All rights reserved worldwide. www.zondervan.com The "NIV" and "New International Version" are trademarks registered in the United States Patent and Trademark Office by Biblica, Inc.™

Scripture references marked KJV are taken from the *King James Version* of the Bible.

Scripture references marked NLT are taken from the *New Living Translation* of the Bible.

Scripture references marked NASB are taken from the *New American Standard Bible,* © 1960, 1963, 1968, 1971, 1972, 1973, 1975, 1977, 1995, 2020 by The Lockman Foundation. Used by permission.

Library of Congress Control Number: 2023905588

Paperback ISBN-13: 978-1-6628-7503-8
Ebook ISBN-13: 978-1-6628-7505-2
Audiobook ISBN-13: 978-1-6628-7506-9

ENDORSEMENTS

A warrior, a statesman, a defender, and a friend, Mike Morrell is an exceptional man who has learned to seek the Lord for God's will and wisdom regarding his and his family's future. Mike has faithfully served in the California State Legislature in Sacramento as well as in his community. He has a great passion and love for history, and his heart beats for his love of country.

After much prayer, Mike realized that the true value of life is not in what you own or possess but rather in the character qualities and integrity one leaves his family. Mike's journey has not always been easy, and in this inspirational book, he will show you how he persevered and stayed the course. I am honored to call Mike Morrell a brother in the faith.

Jack Hibbs,
Senior Pastor of Calvary Chapel
Chino Hills, California

As a pastor of nearly four decades in Southern California, I greatly appreciated Senator Morrell's voice in Sacramento. I had the privilege of knowing Mike for all ten of the years he served in our State Legislature, and I always appreciated his strong, values-based stand for Californians.

As the title of this book suggests, Mike has real insight into the home as the building block of society. He understands how vital strong families are to healthy communities and a prosperous society and nation. This book is filled with good, solid, common-sense advice forged through experience as a husband and father. Its topics of moral excellence, the home, education, finances, leadership, and patriotism are well chosen and have the added weight of a father writing to his children. The wisdom shared in these pages will help young adults and those anywhere in between.

Dr. Paul Chappell,
Senior Pastor of Lancaster Baptist Church
and President of West Coast Baptist College,
Lancaster, California

It was such an honor to have my dear friend and Senate colleague ask me to write encouragement for his book, *The Road to Restoring the Family.*

Mike's book is evidence that God works all things out together for the good for those of us who love him and are called according to His purpose.

It's a book of truth from a biblical standpoint and constructional standpoint that defines and protects the Godly family structure and the constitutional freedoms guaranteed by our founding fathers.

Mike has put together a very thoughtful and well-written book on saving the family, which, in turn, will save America, using biblical principles, family values, and constitutional scholars. Wisdom unfolds at every chapter.

This book is a must-read.

Shannon Grove,
CA State Senator, 12th District

Senator Morrell (RET) served in the California Legislature for ten years. I appreciate his commitment to faith, family, and freedom. I recommend his book. It is timely common-sense advice during these turbulent times for parents and young adults on how to restore the family, the very foundation for a strong America.

Tony Perkins,
Family Research Council

This book is a memoir that is tenderhearted and touching. Mike filled these pages with an authentic introspection about his and his beloved Joanie's life and wise exhortations to his children. Readers will get a glimpse into Senator Morrell's family and life devotions. This story will be an enduring comfort for the fatherless, a timeless companion for fathers, and an equipping book in wisdom for all. It is a beautiful work that shows the turning of a father's heart toward his children and the turning of a father's heart towards his Father in Heaven.

Victoria Lynn PonTell,
RN, PhD

I have known Mike Morrell for more than thirty years. Like all good people, he strives to grow and improve. He has always been determined. In this book, he describes how he learned what he should be determined to do. In mapping out his own life, he provides a guide by which we can live our own. It is a good book, beneficial to anyone who reads it attentively.

Dr. Larry P. Arnn,
President of Hillsdale College

Senator Mike Morrell's wisdom...takes deep complex principles and boils them down to their essence – strong families, caring and connected communities, and a virtuous, prosperous, powerful and free nation!

Len Munsil, B.S., J.D.
President of Arizona Christian University

FOREWORD

· · · · ·

ON DEC 6, 2010 (my dad's birthday) Mike Morrell and I were sworn into the California State Assembly as brand new Assemblymembers. We were seatmates and shared a Bible to take our Oath of Office. Thankfully, Mike's wife Joanie was able to take a picture to memorialize the occasion, and I still display that photo in my office today. We later served together in the California Senate.

Mike's and my friendship began six months prior to our swearing-in, in June, when we both were the surprise winners in our respective primaries. We were elected with several other Christians committed to defending our heritage and fighting for our Judeo-Christian culture. As our group became more comfortable with each other and learned each other's strengths and talents, Mike quickly became known as a prayer warrior. In fact, I (with the approval of the others) appointed him the unofficial Freshman class chaplain.

Mike is diving deep into Abraham Kuyper's "sphere authority" with *The Road to Restoring the Family*. Kuyper wrote "There is not one square inch in the whole domain of our human existence over which Christ, who is Sovereign over all, does not cry, Mine!". That domain is divided into four governments: self, family, church, and state. As believers, we are called to intentionally endeavor to control ourselves in each realm. Mike is giving us a playbook here to lead ourselves, our families, our congregations, and our government to **pursue** perfection in each realm.

Christ has knit Mike's and my heart together, and I am thankful that Mike has taken the time to share his experiences and wisdom in this book.

I agree with him wholeheartedly, and I cannot wait to give each one of my kids a copy, adding my own personal inscription, to encourage them as they begin to get married and start families of their own. My prayer for you is that you will be encouraged, and apply the wisdom and lessons to your life too.

Senator Brian W. Jones
California Senate Minority Leader

PREFACE

. . . . . .

THE PURPOSE OF my life has been guided by the wisdom of King Solomon. In Proverbs 13:22, he wrote that, "A good man leaves an inheritance for their children's children."

Since terming out of the California State Senate, I've considered "what's next?" Thus, my book, *The Road to Restoring the Family*, was born. A strong family will make for a strong America. This is my best attempt to lay out sound solutions in manners spiritually, morally, educationally and politically through my best and earnest take that addresses families of our Nation...alongside my own children.

Today America faces many serious challenges. Anxiety runs deep. Mothers and fathers are searching for answers. The last book, I recall, which stirred a movement back to the family was published over 30 years ago (in 1989), called *Dr. Dobson: Turning Hearts Toward Home* by Rolf Zettersten.[45] It's time again! Prayerfully, *The Road to Restoring the Family: Leaving an Inheritance to Our Children's Children* will be what American families need.

TABLE OF CONTENTS

· · · · ·

ACKNOWLEDGMENTS

· · · · ·

I AM INCREDIBLY grateful to God for His grace and mercy. I thank Him daily for the Godly wife He gave me. As Proverbs 31:12 says, *"She brings him good, not harm, all the days of her life."* My number-one cheerleader, Joanie Morrell, has fulfilled this and more, and I am so thankful. I'm grateful for my children—Kristen, David, Matthew, and Christopher—for their commitment to God, family, and country. They bring so much joy into our lives, and a father could not be more pleased.

I owe a debt of gratitude to the mentors who have invested in my life over the years. Thank you to my spiritual mentors, Pastors Ray Schmauz, Bruce Erickson, and Jack Hibbs. I am deeply grateful to my political mentor, Dr. Larry P. Arnn, the president of Hillsdale College. Dr. Arnn first instructed me about the principles of a limited constitutional government and also mentored two of our sons, David and Matthew. I want to thank the president of Arizona Christian University, Len Munsil, for inviting me to serve as a member of the ACU Board of Trustees. I appreciate ACU's commitment to fighting for its constitutional rights, including the ability to teach and operate according to biblical principles. I also want to thank my business consultant, Gary Lockwood, for helping me to discover how to be a successful business owner.

The following individuals have impacted my life in so many meaningful ways: Tom Frantz, Steve PonTell, Dennis Stockhausen, Tim and Cheryl Aday, Bob Tourse, Alex Espinoza, Nick Calero, and my friend from high school, Rich Macaluso. I especially want to thank Roger Ruvolo for his help, direction, and wise counsel for this book.

I also want to express a gratitude of "thanks" to Taisiya Tveretinova, who heartily shared her time, talents, and much-needed insight in making this book better. I am grateful for her help and her commitment to faith and family.

I want to thank our son, David Morrell, and his friend, Hans Zeiger, for their edits, which helped form and shape this book. And finally, to my wife Joanie: your wise counsel and tireless encouragement helped me not only to write this book but to live the principles contained in it. From my heart, thank you.

INTRODUCTION

· · · · · ·

To my children:

I WRITE THIS book for many reasons. The life verse that was passed on to me many years ago was from Proverbs 13:22, the wisdom of Solomon: "*A good man leaveth an inheritance to his children's children*" (KJV). Allow me to explain how I arrived at that.

I started out in a home that was not Christian. I had good parents, although they had some struggles with alcoholism, which also became a vice of mine, in my late teens and early twenties. We weren't required to go to church, and I don't think we even had a Bible. There were some good, common-sense things my dad instilled into me about paying my bills, not going into debt, and patriotism and love for country. I got into a bit of trouble growing up—a school principal once told me that my name one day would not be Morrell but "Mud." Truthfully, I wasn't the worst kid in school, but I did have my share of drinking, carousing, and getting into trouble.

At twenty-one, I thought about Heaven and Hell. I hoped that I would go to Heaven, but I believed that I was doomed and would be condemned to Hell. I held these thoughts without any knowledge of the Scriptures. I wasn't even sure who that guy was on the cross. That's how devoid I was of any kind of spirituality.

Then, one day I was invited to hear a talk by a pastor named Ray Schmautz, who had previously been a linebacker for the Oakland Raiders.

I don't recall what he said, but I remember my soul crying out to God that I needed Him. Something transitioned in my life where I knew very clearly that I needed God. Things started to happen. Ray Schmautz mentored me and would call me and ask me what Scriptures I had read. I grew through this. God began to transform my life—not overnight—but I was on a journey of grace that continues to this day.

On the dating scene, I started asking a few of the women at church who they thought the most spiritual college-age girl was. Three times, the name Joanie Laliberte came back to me. A fourth time, Pastor Schmautz asked me, "Have you ever thought of taking out Joanie Laliberte on a date?"

I said, "No, I don't even know what she looks like."

"Well, she's in the back of the room," he replied. I looked at her, and she had the longest, shiniest black hair, and she was beautiful. I asked her out, and eleven months later, we got married.

I didn't want kids. They cost money, they require time, and I was not into that. Joanie wanted kids.

What I didn't appreciate at the time was that God cares more about these little ones than Mike Morrell does. Even though I was a worrier and worked hard, God met me every step of the way. It took me a while to realize it, but God was carrying the burden the whole time. God cared for and loved my children - Kristen, David, Matthew, and Chris - more than I ever could. It never was as tough as I thought it would be. He allowed us to make enough money to save, provide for our kids, and fulfill Joanie's desire to stay at home and make her kids the number-one priority in her life.

I once took a three-day class on the seven deadly sins. The great religious philosophers said that these seven sins would tank a man or woman, and they would cause them to become ensnared in other sins. One sin would lead to another. Many scholars have said that slothfulness is the deadliest sin. It's not just being lazy, but it's laziness of spirit. In his *The Summa Theologica*, St. Thomas Aquinas said that *"sloth is sluggishness of the mind which neglects to begin good...is evil in its effect if it so oppresses man as to draw him away entirely from good deeds.*"[2] Great achievers like Lincoln and Churchill were distinguished by their convictions.

I do not want my kids or grandchildren to live a life of neutrality. I want you to live a life that is distinguished by your principles, convictions, and courage.

In this book, I pass my thoughts on to you: my mistakes, lessons, experiences, and victories. I do this in the light of God's Word and with a deep reliance on the wisdom of others whose writings and lessons have given me inspiration over the decades. And I do this in the hope that I might inspire you in your own pursuit of principles, convictions, and courage.

I have tried to write from the truths contained in Scripture as well as the "laws of nature and of nature's God," which are "self-evident" in the ordering of the universe, in history, and in human nature, to borrow an idea from the Declaration of Independence. Together, this forms a dual foundation of faith and reason. In America, we could say that the best of Jerusalem, the home of faith, came together with the best of Athens, the home of reason. I have tried to stand on the shoulders of people who possessed the spirit of wisdom by learning from people like Aristotle, Plato, Cato, Thomas Aquinas, John Locke, John Adams, and Samuel Adams, as well as the wisdom contained in the Scriptures and written by people like Paul, Timothy, and the Old Testament writers.

When I was a young man, an older gentleman could see me struggling and suggested that I read a chapter of Proverbs every day of the month. There are typically thirty-one days in the month and there are thirty-one chapters in the book. I began reading a chapter a day for each day of the month. If the day were the 24th, I would read Proverbs 24. It takes approximately two minutes to read a chapter. I could read through the Proverbs every month the rest of my life. It wouldn't take much time out of my day, and I would gain wisdom this way, I was told.

I have truly learned to love the Proverbs. In them, I have found the keys to financial wisdom, how to deal with people, how to have a successful marriage, how to raise children, when to discipline and not to discipline, and how to distinguish folly from wisdom. As a man or woman reads the Proverbs, they will grow in their relationships, their role as a servant and leader, and gain insight on how to increase their chances of attaining prosperity—one of my favorite subjects.

I have tried to incorporate principles like these into this book so that I can pass along some of the wisdom that has guided me in my relationships and decisions and given me a sense of purpose and meaning. But more importantly, my intention is that I want to give you the best advice possible because I want you to prosper in every way possible.

When I first encountered Proverbs 13:22—*"A good man leaves an inheritance for their children's children"*—I thought that the calling contained in the verse was not much of a calling. I took it in part to mean money. I didn't think God required me to leave a whole lot of money to my children, so it wasn't awe-inspiring to me. It took me a couple of years to realize that an inheritance goes beyond financial considerations: it extends to education, morality, civic responsibility, and family responsibilities. Eventually, this verse took on a completely new meaning.

I worked hard to provide for your schooling as well as your college, and I did what I could to be involved in the community during my years in business. I started some Christian ministries with my friend Steve PonTell. Then, when Matthew left and went away to college, I ran and was elected as Assemblyman in the California State Legislature, serving out my civic responsibility in a more meaningful way. What I lost in annual income in balancing my various responsibilities, I gained in a true inheritance that I could leave to my children. It is better to live modestly with a life well spent than to earn lots of money having shirked our duties.

As your father and grandfather, I had the responsibility to begin the process of your education. Although I did my best, I was limited in some factors and have realized that there are things I could have done better. Now that you are grown and have children of your own, you have learned lessons of your own, and your education has surpassed my own in many ways. I have watched you begin to pass along wisdom to your own kids. I hope you may find that my reflections affirm (or reaffirm) your own understanding of things. You may take some interest in knowing how I have attempted to summarize the major themes of the life we have shared.

I began writing this book to my children. I took some time off, mostly because of my commitments during my years in the Legislature. Today, I write because I want to pass this on to my grandchildren and their children yet to be born. It's the duty of a father to leave an inheritance; thus, I am writing this book.

One key piece of advice to take note of is to take life seriously, but do not take yourself too seriously. In this chaotic world, we are reminded in the book of Proverbs 14:30 that *"A heart at peace gives life to the body, but envy rots the bones."* So as we face these serious issues of our day, work on having a cheerful disposition, always looking for the good in life, with a heart full of thanks to our loving God.

Here is my best attempt to lay out the things that are important to me, including faith, morality, family, business, finances, citizenship, and what we must do to save our country (a hint: if we want to save our country, we must begin by saving our families, consisting of fathers and mothers raising kids who are going to love God and their country and their fellow citizens). This is the inheritance I am trying to leave to the next generation. May you be blessed in reading the pages that follow, and may God bless you and your children and your children's children.

Love,
Dad

Rancho Cucamonga, California

I.

THE ROAD TO MORAL EXCELLENCE AND GRACIOUS LIVING

· · · · · ·

Dear Children,

PERHAPS THE MOST important part of success—both physical and spiritual—is the act of becoming virtuous or possessing virtue within yourself. What, then, is virtue?

This question has been asked for over three thousand years. Philosophers and theologians such as Socrates, Plato, Aristotle, Cicero, Virgil, Augustine, Aquinas, and many others, have thought it so worthwhile that they dedicated much of their lives, not only to understanding virtue but also to becoming virtuous. In their estimation, virtue is a condition of the soul. It comes as a result of training and many years of right choices that actually change the character of the soul. For example, if one constantly overeats, they will become an overeater. Likewise, if one always chooses moderation in food and drink, they will become moderate and have the virtue of moderation. If a person chooses to act justly, then they will become just. You see, our actions actually change our souls—both for better and worse. This is why virtue is important; we become what we do.

1

And it so happens that once a pattern of action, a quality of the soul, is established, it is very difficult, though not impossible, to change it. This is why we must constantly choose virtue over vice: right over wrong.

In addition, while virtue is good for the soul because it represents a fulfillment of what a person was made to be, it also will directly influence and shape how effective of a person you become in life. In fact, author Stephen Covey, in his book, *The Seven Habits of Highly Effective People*, found that while most business and self-help books written over the past fifty years have focused on superficial ideas (like techniques and image consciousness), comparable literature written one hundred years prior focused not on the surface qualities, but rather on the inner characteristics of a person: on ethics, integrity, humility, temperance, patience, and the golden rule.[11] These authors saw that one cannot succeed in life without paying great attention to virtue. They believed that virtues were of utmost importance because they were the qualities that would make a person successful, not just financially, but in the most complete sense of well-being.

Think of it this way: describe a good chair. It is well-assembled; it is sturdy; it is made from a hard wood; it has a backrest; and above all, it does what it is supposed to do: hold a person up who sits upon it. In other words, what makes a good chair is simply the quality of it doing what it is supposed to do. All of the characteristics mentioned before serve this purpose. These characteristics are the "virtues" of the chair.

In the same way, a virtuous human being is one who simply does what she or he was made to do. The qualities that are a part of this person—who does what they were made to do—would be the virtues. Consequently, virtue is simply the qualities that allow us to be what we are supposed to be at our best and highest potential. They aim for the good life.

In fact, in classical thought (from which most of our ideas of virtue originated), virtues were defined as good habits that keep people both; from swerving from the straight and true, and on the path to our final destiny. Virtue is the highest principle of human action, which plays a part in our rational, spiritual, and supernatural development. It is the existence of a finely shaped human spirit in the context of our character.

So what are the actual virtues? Well, it turns out that there are many. The classical thinkers identified four cardinal or key virtues: moderation, justice, fortitude, and prudence. Christian thinkers like Augustine and Aquinas, while accepting as key these four virtues, also identified three other key theological virtues: faith, hope, and love. For them, these seven virtues were of utmost importance for the human soul and its relationship to God and fellow man. And they believed that, precisely speaking, it was impossible to be virtuous in one area and lack it in another. In other words, to have one virtue means that you must have all of the virtues. So, you might say: then is virtue impossible on Earth? The strict answer is "yes." However, since virtues are not like light switches that are either turned on or off, one can possess them to greater or lesser extents. This means that, though we will never be perfect on Earth, we are called to *pursue perfection*, to approximate the high standard that has been set for us. And here are some of the other areas in which we should do this:

Peace	Piety	Duty
Joy	Reverence	Gratitude
Thankfulness	Truthfulness	Honesty
Kindness	Courtesy	Service
Diligence	Excellence	Wholesomeness
Honor	Sacrifice	Industry
Compassion	Patience	

It is important to note that though virtue is desirable and good for the human soul, a commitment to one virtue at the expense of the other can have bad results. For example, if a person of justice lacks mercy, they can become a person of cruelty. So, for justice to be a virtue, it must be balanced by mercy and compassion. Another example would be a person of compassion who lacks courage and becomes a coward. Both courage and compassion must be joined for virtue to be present.

Since it would take a separate book to cover all of the virtues, I will focus on the ones I believe are most critical to success. The first is industry, which is defined as *diligent activity directed toward some purpose*. It was for much time widely believed that industry was a moral duty that people have and a way of obtaining the blessings of Heaven. Essentially, industry comes down to hard work. Next is perseverance, whose brother is persistence. The difference between the two is that persistence has an external focus and perseverance, an internal one. Both, however, require strength. Both play a part in overcoming the inevitable and difficult circumstances of life, which are essential to prevail over for success. Perseverance is about not giving up and *always* getting up after getting knocked down.

Another virtue is that of discipline, which comes from the Latin verb meaning "to educate," (translated by author). Benjamin Franklin believed that the majority of success comes from one being disciplined in their work. If one is lazy, they will miss out on opportunities for success. As Franklin wrote in his essay "The Way to Wealth," "Sloth, like rust, consumes faster than labor wears, while the used key is always bright."

Next, moderation is important to combine with discipline and perseverance, so one will not become a workaholic and lose his family by spending too many hours at the office. **Moderation** requires a healthy soul to keep us from excess. It also helps us to avoid the immoral desires that lead to ruin.

The virtue of prudence is among the most important for business and politics. In short, prudence is the ability to apply moral virtue and knowledge to circumstances. It is the practical virtue. It decides how to be moderate, when to be courageous, where to be merciful, and so on. It is about timing, manner, and situations. Prudence involves judgment and lends foresight. It is the virtue of the wise counselor. Without prudence, all of the virtues are impossible. While the moral virtues are about ends, prudence is about choosing the appropriate means to get there.

Charity is the great Christian virtue. The Greek word is *agape* and means *an unlimited loving-kindness to others* (translated by author). People who are generous have unlimited loving-kindness toward all. It flows out of an awareness that everything we have is from God. Psalm 24:1 says, *"The Earth is the Lord's, and everything in it, the world, and all who live in it."*

As we grow in charity, we gain clear-sightedness of what the important things are. In the *Confessions of St. Augustine* publication from the Anno Domini (A.D.) period, St. Augustine believed that since God is the Giver of all good gifts, as our parents give us life and nurture us, we owe a debt to God and others. Part of this debt is through charity. Since God loved us and sent His son to die for us, it is clear that God has shown perfect charity to us. Therefore, we should keep things such as this in mind to help us keep a charitable spirit.

The next virtue is contentment. The virtue of contentment is the acquiescence of the mind to the lot God has given. It takes a Godly and patient person to be content. When we are content, we avoid covetousness. We will not be envious when one of our friends or neighbors is prosperous because we are content with what God has given us. Apostle Paul said he learned to be content with little, as well as with much. There is nothing wrong with ambition as long as it is tempered and not driven out to discontent.

In addition, the virtue of humility is important because it keeps us from becoming prideful. Humility is the antidote to pride. God resists the proud but gives grace to the humble. Humility reminds us of our limitations and need for reliance upon God. Proverbs 16:18 says, *"Pride goeth before destruction, and an haughty spirit before a fall"* (KJV). Humility is one of the most difficult for us men. We, above all, need to keep our pride in check.

The last virtue—which is not exactly a virtue but an important disposition in life—is merriment. Remember that there is always a downside to constant seriousness. It causes us to worry. Therefore, it is good to have fun, to have a light-hearted disposition. As Proverbs 17:22 says, *"A cheerful heart is good medicine."* Ecclesiastes 3:8 confirms this statement as it says that while there is a time for war and a time for peace, there is also a time to play. Life is too short and too comical to never smile and laugh. In fact, laughter, merriment, and joy are important parts of the human life. As G. K. Chesterton wrote in his 1908 book *All Things Considered*, *"It might reasonably be maintained that the true object of human life is play. Earth is a task garden; Heaven is a playground."* If that is the case, then let the play begin!

Work can be a lot more fun…if you do not look at it as a weight and burden. Do not spend your life waiting for Friday. Rather, enjoy every day as it comes, for there is plenty to enjoy in each one. If you are constantly looking forward to things to come, you will miss the wonders and joys right before your eyes.

If you do not believe this, look at the evidence for these contentions in *The Millionaire Next Door* by Thomas J. Stanley and William D. Danko.[13] These two authors, after years of studying the financial habits of both millionaires and non-millionaires, found some interesting things: often, people with big homes on tops of big hills who drive big, expensive cars…have big debt. On the other hand, they found that most millionaires lived frugal lives on average and had unpretentious homes, while driving average cars.

Here are some traits that I have observed millionaires often exhibit:

1. They live below their means. They are frugal. I guess you could make a case that they exhibit the virtues of discipline, sacrifice, wisdom, and perhaps humility.
2. They allocate their time and energy to work effectively and efficiently as they accumulate wealth. The virtues that come to mind are industry, perseverance, and, again, wisdom.
3. Their parents did not provide economic outpatient care for them. They make it on their own. They are responsible, hardworking people.

These millionaires had average to above-average incomes. What made them millionaires, though, was that they learned to keep debt low, make money, and save it. Their motivation for this was to "buy" time and "spend" it with family. Take their example and put your life in its proper order.

But I finish with the thought that the highest things to pursue are Godly purpose and Godly beauty. Only then will you truly succeed, and your life will be well spent.

Love,
Dad

II.

GRATITUDE

· · · · ·

"Be thankful unto Him and bless His name."

—Psalm 100:4 (KJV)

"Therefore, I will give thanks unto Thee."

—2 Samuel 22:50 (KJV)

"I will give thanks unto Thee forever."

—Psalm 30:12 (KJV)

"Give praise to the Lord, proclaim His name; make known among the nations what He has done." —Psalm 105:1

"Give thanks to the Lord, for He is good; His love endures forever."

—Psalm 106:1

"At midnight I will rise to give You thanks for Your righteous laws."

—Psalm 119:62

"Instead, be filled with the Spirit, speaking to one another with psalms, hymns and songs from the Spirit. Sing and make music from your heart to the Lord, always giving thanks to God the Father for everything, in the name of our Lord Jesus Christ." —Ephesians 5:18–20

"Rejoice always, pray continually, give thanks in all circumstances; for this is God's will for you in Christ Jesus." —1 Thessalonians 5:16–18

Dear Children,

THE POINT IN all of these Scripture passages is clear and simple: give thanks. Everything you have has been given to you, and because of this, we have a duty to offer our appreciation and gratitude to the giver. The ultimate giver of all things, of course, is God.

It is often easy, however, to make excuses for our lack of gratitude in difficult times. We feel justified in not giving thanks simply because things have not gone our way. We should always be thankful for the simple reason that there are always things to be thankful for – even if those things don't fulfill our checklists. Life itself is a gift. We should not forget this. In all things, give thanks. Even the worst circumstances might very well be a blessing in disguise, times in our lives that will help us grow into better human beings. And this sometimes requires pain. In the end, however, we can rest assured that it is all part of God's infinitely loving plan for us.

In my life, I have had times when I have become discouraged over bad things that have happened. And at times, it is okay to be feel down. It is a valid emotion. Bad things happen in this world that merit our sorrow— accidents, losing family members, injury, and others. But I have also noticed that when little things in life do not go my way sometimes, I get worried. Over what? In the scope of all things considered, it's often the miniscule ones that count the most to us. This is not right. But by faith, I have learned to be thankful. I even tell God that I do not feel like giving thanks at this particular time, but I will anyhow because I remember His faithfulness. Even this has helped me change my negative mindset into a positive one.

Our minds are often like computers—data in, data out. If you think negatively, you will become negative and view life accordingly. But if you think positively, you will become positive. It will help you move out of the depressing situations more quickly. It also honors God and is a good testimony to others. So count your blessings. Have a good attitude. We see too many whiners and complainers today. My dad, a World War II veteran of the "greatest generation," never used terms like "I'm stressed" or "depressed." These are new phrases. Try not to complain over the trivial.

Consider Moses as an example of why not to complain. Multiple times in the book of Exodus, God tells Moses to go to Pharaoh and say, *"Let my people go!"* When he does this, Pharaoh says, "No." God then begins to perform miracles. He takes Aaron's staff, and it becomes a snake. The Pharaoh's heart is hardened to the idea of letting the Israelites go. So God speaks to Moses again and says:

"Pharaoh's heart is unyielding; he refuses to let my people go. Go to Pharaoh in the morning as he goes out to the river. Confront him on the bank of the Nile, and take in your hand the staff that was changed into a snake. Then say to him, 'The Lord, the God of the Hebrews, has sent me to say to you: Let my people go, so that they may worship me in the wilderness. But until now you have not listened. This is what the Lord says: By this you will know that I am the Lord: With the staff that is in my hand I will strike the water of the Nile, and it will be changed into blood. The fish in the Nile will die, and the river will stink; the Egyptians will not be able to drink its water'" (Exod. 7:14–18).

God did this. The water turned to blood and poured over the streams, canals, and into the ponds. All the reservoirs were turned to blood everywhere in Egypt. Even the people's water in wooden buckets was turned to blood.

> *"Seven days passed and then the Lord said to Moses, 'Go to Pharaoh and say to him, "This is what the Lord says: Let my people go, so that they may worship Me"'".*   (Exod. 8:1).

Pharaoh refuses again. And then God begins to strike Egypt with different plagues.

Now think about this. If you are a Hebrew watching these miracles, you should be praising God as you see His power. And this is just the beginning. Moses keeps going back to Pharaoh, performing the Lord's miracle after miracle that the Hebrews are seeing. Each time Moses goes to Pharaoh after one of these plagues, he says, *"Let My people go."*

And again, Pharaoh says, "No." Then God performs the miracle with the plague of the gnats, the plague of the flies, the plague of the livestock, the plague of the boils, the plague of hail, and the Death of the Firstborn. Time after time, God performs miracles for the Israelites. And then, finally, there is the plague of the death of the firstborn in every family. And then Pharaoh says, *"Up! Leave my people, you and the Israelites!"* (Exod. 12:31).

Then God makes them a promise in Exodus 13 and tells the Israelites this, *"When the Lord brings you into the land of the Canaanites, Hittites, Amorites, Hivites and Jebusites—the land He swore to your ancestors to give you, a land flowing with milk and honey—you are to observe this ceremony in the month"* (Exod. 13:5).

God not only frees the Israelites from bondage after hundreds of years, but He also promises them a land flowing with milk and honey. Yet as the Israelites begin to leave Egypt and cross the Red Sea, Pharaoh goes back on his promise and pursues after them with his army, saying, *"We have let the Israelites go and have lost their services!"* (Exod. 14:5).

With his army and chariots, Pharaoh pursues the Israelites, and as he approaches them, the Israelites become terrified and cry out to the Lord. Even after seeing all of the previous miracles done for their sake, the Israelites ask Moses, "*Was it because there were no graves in Egypt that you brought us here to the desert to die? What have you done to us bringing us out of Egypt? Didn't we say to you in Egypt, 'leave us alone, let us serve the Egyptians'? It would have been better for us to have served the Egyptians than to die in the desert!*" (Exod. 14:11–12).

As they encounter trials, they are immediately ready to give up. They forget God's promises. So Moses reminds them in Exodus 14:14, "*The Lord will fight for you; you need only to be still.*" And as God leads them across the Red Sea, He parts it for them. The Egyptian army pursues and is soon covered with a sea of water.

Shortly afterward, the Israelites are in the desert for a few days, and they begin to complain and grumble again. As Exodus 15:24 says, "*So the people grumbled against Moses, saying, 'What are we to drink?'*" Moses cries out to the Lord, asking for "help." And God provides water for them out of the rocks—another miracle. Then, in Exodus 16:3, they are complaining to Moses and Aaron, saying, "*If only we had died by the Lord's hand in Egypt! There we sat around pots of meat and ate all the food we wanted, but you have brought us out into this desert to starve this entire assembly to death.*"

God responds by raining down food from Heaven called *manna*. It should be no surprise, though, that they soon recommence their grumbling because they are tired of the manna. God then rains down quail from Heaven—another miracle. But each time things get tough, they grumble. And not only do they grumble, but they also forget God's promises. They even make idols and worship them instead of God.

The moral of the story is this: while grumbling and complaining, one will forget all that God has done. In fact, complaining is a way of saying that we have already forgotten all of the wonderful things God has done for us. It is a slap in the face to God and a rejection of all that He has graciously provided us.

In addition, this is a lesson in the folly of dependence on the government. God wants us to be free, yet the Israelites were under the delusion that it would be better to return to slavery than to keep faith in God's promises. They lost sight of the big picture, and they grew weary of the reality that freedom comes with a lot of hard work—and faith.

Let's explore how this relates to finances. Finances are a big part of our daily lives, and it is easy to worry that God won't provide. Many people do, in fact, worry about money—as I have, many times. Issues relating to money are one of the top reasons for divorce. So it is good to be mindful that God, in fact, does provide. Remember His faithfulness from past experiences, taking time to give praise rather than complaint. Remember, when I was young, I encountered one of the worst real estate markets of my career. And I am reminded now how faithful God was to me at that time; He made sufficient provision for me and my family. Even as I have complained, God has always taken care of me. We have never gone without food, water, or shelter. He has provided in spectacular ways. Above all, I am especially grateful that my Kristen, Matt, David, and Chris are walking with the Lord as His children – which fills me with pure joy that they are my children. Thus, we must, as the saying goes, "Have an attitude of gratitude."

In addition, God often provides for our material needs before we even ask. He knows our needs, and if we seek Him, He will help us to fill them. This is why we must not let complaining become a pattern in life. You may, like the Israelites, end up wandering in your own desert for forty years. So, in good times or bad, peaks or valleys, try to keep it all in perspective, remembering all the past glorious things He has done for you. The history of the Israelites is there for us to learn from their mistakes and reminds us of God's faithfulness. We must not forget these lessons, but rather we should always remember God's graciousness and work towards a habit of thankfulness. A quote published in *The Wisdom and Teachings of Stephen R. Covey* says this: *"Sow a thought, and you reap an act; sow an act, and you reap a habit; sow a habit, and you reap a character; sow a character, and you reap a destiny."*[12] In the book, these words are attributed to George Dana Boardman (as a more recent account) but have actually originated long beforehand. This quote has linked one's thought to one's destiny for over a century, being associated with educator Charlotte Manson, novelist William Makepeace Thackeray, and most popularly, essayist Ralph Waldo Emerson. Even today, it is still not clear as to who initially spoke these words of wisdom, which goes to show that true teachings are timeless: popular then, relevant now, and pertinent always. Likewise, submit to God and ask Him to help you during trials. As the apostle says in 2 Corinthians 4:8, 9, and 16, "*We are hard pressed on every side, but not crushed; perplexed, but not in despair; persecuted, but not abandoned; struck down, but not destroyed . . . Therefore, we do not lose heart.*"

Remember all the great and wonderful things God has done. Do not be discontented but rather be thankful for every gift you have. And when the going gets tough, do not be like the many who make excuses because they are down or the Hebrews who complained about the leadership of Aaron and Moses. Instead, be introspective when things go wrong and ask whether or not others are really the cause of your problems. Ask whether or not it could be you or just those normal bumps in life.

Do not be like those who complain and run from problems. Sometimes problems are opportunities for success. For example, a professional baseball player for the New York Yankees, Jim Abbott, pitched a no-hitter against Cleveland on September 4, 1993.[38] He played for ten seasons on four different teams. Today, he is a pitching instructor for the Los Angeles Angels. What makes him unique is he does not have a right hand. He battled against the odds and succeeded, not ever wanting to give up.

So, regardless of your lot in life, praise God. I have been told that whatever doesn't kill you will usually make you stronger. So just walk by faith, trust in God, and be thankful.

Love,
Dad

KEY TAKEAWAY

Be thankful, even when things don't go your way.

III.

PRAYER & QUIET REFLECTIONS

· · · · · ·

Dear Children,

PRAYER SHOULD BE a central part of your life. Even if your motives for praying are not always perfect, still ask God for what you need—protection, help, a decent living. He understands our weaknesses and desires when we offer them up to Him in prayer.

In my own life, I have learned the power of prayer firsthand. For many years, I have made it a priority to take my concerns—even my material ones—to Him daily. Though I perhaps ask for too many things, I continue to pray and hope that God will give me what I need and keep me away from evil. I encourage you do the same. He will limit what you can have and give you what you need. I have found that prayer is essential for our well-being. This was especially true as I worked in a very dangerous place: the California State Legislature. Prayer kept me going, protected me, opened doors, and gave me strength to say no when I needed it.

Christ spent much time in prayer. For example, in John 6:14–15, we see Christ feeding the five-thousand. When He is done ministering there, healing, and preaching to them, the Scripture says, *"After the people saw* the sign Jesus performed, they began to say, 'Surely, this is the Prophet who is to come into the world.' Jesus, knowing that they intended to come and make Him King by force, withdrew again to a mountain by Himself." Notice it says that He withdrew again...by Himself. "Again" means He had done this before. It is not an isolated event:

- John 11:54 says, "[H]e withdrew to a region near the desert."
- Luke 5:16 says, "But He Himself would often slip away to the wilderness and pray" (NASB).
- Luke 6:12 says, "It was at this time that He went off to the mountain to pray, and He spent the whole night in prayer to God" (NASB).

The same thing happens in Matthew 14:20–24. Many times after doing His ministry, Christ would retreat into the wilderness to spend time with the Father. Christ had a need to spend time with the Father. If even He needed this, how much more time should we, frail humans, spend with our Father?

I know I certainly have needed time to pray. Many times I had become busy with work, the employees I had to manage, legislative duties, family, and church. I had deadlines and bottom lines to worry about. Then, in addition to these responsibilities, I had to plan for the future, my children's college education, my retirement, and my reelection. After a while, it became a fast-paced merry-go-round. I soon developed tunnel vision and lost my focus. Then the worries overwhelmed me. I became ineffective. This is when I needed downtime with God to contemplate.

In fact, many business consultants will tell you that people are most creative and effective when their minds are relaxed. These people do not talk in terms of prayer but rather in terms of needing to get away to clear their thoughts, to relax the mind, to have peace. They say that when we have downtime, we become more creative. Our thinking is restored.

In the same way, we need time for quiet reflection with God; it is essential for our souls to be in communion with the Father.

Secular studies have shown the benefits of quiet time and meditation. For example, an article in *The Journal of Behavioral Medicine* compared studies on secular and spiritual forms of meditation in order to understand its benefits.[42] In one study, participants were taught meditation and relaxation techniques and were encouraged to practice them for twenty minutes a day for two weeks. After two weeks, the participants returned to the lab, and researchers found that they had positive moods and decreased anxiety, and they seemed to tolerate pain better than the ones in the group who did not practice relaxation techniques and meditation.

Another experiment (done by the scientists team of D. A. Matthews, M. E. McCullough, D. B. Larsen, H. J. Koenig, J. P. Swyers, and M. G. Milano) in 1998 studied the relationship between people's religious devotion and physical and mental health.[30] They studied factors such as frequency of religious involvement and to what extent people used their spiritual beliefs as a source of strength and coping. Physical and mental health was gauged according to people's ability to prevent, cope with, and recover from illness. The studies found that about 80 percent of the public religious commitment was connected to better health. A Gallup poll came to a similar conclusion when it found that, on average, people who had religious affiliations and beliefs in God had better mental well-being than the non-religious. In 1990, another study assessing 451 people was performed by scientists trio Brown, Gary, and Ndubuisi, who found that men with low religious involvement "scored almost twice as high on the depression scale as their more religious counterparts."[8] Similarly, the 1998 study mentioned above found that prayer and religious commitment also reduced the prospect of mental illnesses. Studies abound in showing the positive effects that prayer has. Prayer has been revealed to be good for our health through proven results of scientific discoveries, and despite receiving minimal attention, these revelations are no less exciting as they are unexpected horizons.

After reviewing these studies, I am beginning to understand why Christ retreated to the wilderness. There are clear benefits to downtime and relaxation. And so, as I have studied, I have found over 500 verses pertaining to prayer throughout the Old and New Testaments. But the one that seems to stick out for me is in Philippians 4:4–7, which says,

> *"Rejoice in the Lord always; again I will say, rejoice! Let your gentle spirit be known to all men. The Lord is near. Be anxious for nothing, but in everything by prayer and supplication with thanksgiving let your request be made known to God. And the peace of God, which surpasses all comprehension, will guard your hearts and your minds in Christ Jesus"* (NASB).

It is wise for us to retreat into our own wilderness—whether it be on a mountaintop, the desert, or a park a couple of miles away from home. It has been most profitable for me. I have found that it allows clarity of thinking and the ability to focus better on the more important matters in life.

So retreat. Take mini vacations as often as you can. I often go to the park with my yellow scratchpad and begin to think about my wife, relationships, children, ministry, my business, and what is next for me in life. I invite God to be part of my thought process. I just begin to think naturally, and in doing so, I have noticed that my spirit calms and my mind relaxes. This is from where some of my best and brightest ideas have sprung forth. Somehow, the creativity flows. Fruit is born in all areas of life—spiritual, mental, and financial. The only question is: Why don't I do it more? On Saturday mornings, your mother and I have often taken our walks for approximately an hour and a half. We discuss life in general and invite God to be a part of our conversation. We just walk and talk to each other and ask God to guide our conversations and thoughts. We ask that God enable us to be better parents, spouses, citizens, employers, and employees. It seems like God has had His hand on us. I cannot overemphasize the power of prayer. Consider these Scriptures:

+ Matthew 21:22: *"If you believe, you will receive whatever you ask for in prayer."*
+ James 5:16: *"Therefore, confess your sins to each other and pray for each other so that you may be healed. The prayer of a righteous person is powerful and effective."*
+ Proverbs 15:8: *"The Lord detests the sacrifice of the wicked, but the prayer of the upright pleases Him."*
+ Proverbs 15:29: *"The Lord is far from the wicked, but He hears the prayer of the righteous."*

But the best prayer is known as our Lord's Prayer, which reminds us to say, *"Thy will be done."* This gets the focus off of us and puts it on what God wants.

So pray. Pray for your family. Pray for our country. Pray for good health. And pray for your finances. You cannot afford not to take time to pray. God will make up any lost time. Avoid that fast-paced merry-go-round I have sometimes found myself on; it is not how life is intended to be. As I reflect back, this has proven to be a winning strategy—to take time to get away from the office or life in general. Short vacations or just a walk to the park are very productive times. Rarely do my best ideas come in the middle of a hurricane.

Next, and more importantly, what a great asset your mother has been as she has – since all of you were in grade school – to show up at your school on Tuesday mornings for an hour and a half on average and pray and seek God for your betterment and education, to grow your soul and protect you physically, mentally, and spiritually, and to pray for your teachers that they would teach the right things and evil would be rebuked in your life. My cup runneth over as I look back on this. How can you even measure the blessings that came from this? We'll only know in Heaven how valuable those prayers are.

I would like to share Matt Morrell's opinion, which attests to the power of his mother's prayers. Matt wrote this in a Damien High School publication during his school years: *"My mom gathered with other moms to pray for sons at Damien. I think we underestimate what goes on in the spiritual realm of life, but I have no doubt those prayers, even to this day, have had major impacts on me and the rest of my family."*

Even here on Earth, I have seen so many prayers answered over the years. I am grateful that I found your mother, who is committed to a consistent prayer life. I encourage you to commit to prayer as well. I know it's tough when you're raising a family and providing for everybody to show up for a couple of hours once a week to pray with other people, but you can do it. Get away from work and take a few minutes here, a few minutes there in the morning, and at night to keep up your connection to God.

Love,
Dad

KEY TAKEAWAYS

Make prayer a priority.

*Prayer nourishes the soul, calms the mind,
and helps avoid depression.*

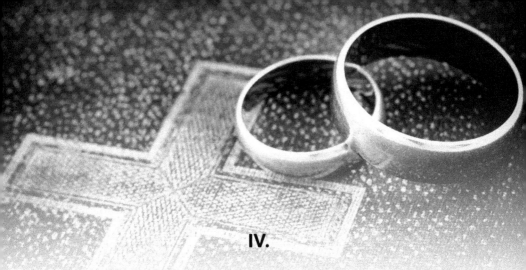

IV.

MARRIAGE & FAMILY—THE CHANNEL OF SANCTIFIED GRACE

. . . . . .

So God created man in His own image, in the image of God He created him; male and female He created them. Then God blessed them and said to them, "Be fruitful and multiply; fill the Earth and subdue it; have dominion over the fish of the sea, over the birds of the air, and over every living thing that moves on the Earth." . . . Therefore, a man shall leave his mother and father and be joined to his wife, and they shall become one flesh.

—Genesis 1:27–28; 2:24

Dear Children,

YOUR LIFE AND well-being depend on choosing the right spouse. So does that of your children and their children. Even the destiny of nations depends on men and women who commit to a life together...so choose wisely.

As Proverbs 31:10 says, *"An excellent wife, who can find? For her worth is far above jewels. The heart of her husband trusts in her and she will have no lack of gain. She does him good and not evil all the days of her life"* (NASB).

Another translation for "excellent wife" is "noble" wife (NIV), as in nobility. It's someone who is morally good, virtuous, superior in nature and character, exalted, grand, and stately. That's the first thing you should look for: a spouse who is noble in character.

It is said that a young woman once approached Benjamin Franklin and asked how she could find a good husband. His answer: *"Become a good woman."* It turns out in marriage, as in other aspects of life, the best unions are those like birds of a feather that flock together. If you want to find a virtuous person to marry, be a virtuous person. Work on your own virtues. Become a person of character and integrity. The best way to find a spouse is to work on your own virtues because you'll reap what you sow. If you are a virtuous person, you'll find a virtuous person.

It is important to choose a Christian to marry, but that's just the start of the criteria you should consider. When you're choosing a spouse, take time to assess their virtues. Look for a person with a depth of commitment to Christ. And remember that marriage is a lifetime commitment, so look before you leap. Ask some basic questions. How do they pay their bills? Do they keep their word to their friends? How do they treat their parents? How do their parents treat them? Did their parents stay married? And most of all—are they consistent with Scripture readings?

Proverbs 31:11 says, *"The heart of her husband trusts in her"* (NASB). You want to find someone who is trustworthy—not just trustworthy to you, but to everyone around her.

Proverbs 31:12 adds, *"She does him good and not evil all the days of her life"* (NASB). If that doesn't happen in dating, it certainly won't happen in marriage.

Verses 14 through 24 talks about her work ethic and generosity. Verse 18 says, *"Her lamp does not go out at night"* (NASB). Verse 20 describes how she extends her hands to the needy. In verses 21 through 25, she is not afraid of snow, for her household is clothed with scarlet. In other words, she is prepared for life's challenges. She has clothes for her children and husband and fine linens so they can lay down at night. Verse 25 says, "*Strength and dignity are her clothing and she smiles at the future*" (NASB).

Note this in verse 26: "*She opens her mouth in wisdom, and the teaching of kindness is on her tongue*" (NASB). She's a woman of wisdom. You want to marry a sharp woman. I don't just mean on an intellectual level. I'm talking about spiritual sharpness. You also want to marry a kind woman.

Verse 27 says, "*She looks well to the ways of her household and does not eat the bread of idleness*" (NASB). She's not a prima donna. She doesn't expect other people to wait on her; rather, she serves others. (Don't take this for granted in your spouse, by the way—be a person who exhibits these same qualities.)

Here are the blessings when a man marries a woman like this: "*Her children rise up and bless her; her husband also, and he praises her, saying, 'Many daughters have done nobly, but you excel them all.' Charm is deceitful and beauty is vain, but a woman who fears the Lord, she shall be praised. Give her the product of her hands and let her works praise her in the gates*" (Prov. 31:28–30 NASB).

Remember that charm is deceitful, and beauty is vain. Another translation says that "*beauty is fleeting*" (NIV). It lasts for a short time. That's why the greatest thing you can find is a woman who fears the Lord. The result is that she will be praised. You, her husband, will rise up and praise her, as will your children. It will be a blessing to the whole family.

So choose the right person, the one who you'll share a home with for years. Choose someone with whom you can produce and bring up children. Martin Luther said in a 1522 sermon titled "Living as Husband and Wife," "*Most certainly, father and mother are apostles, bishops and priests to their children, for it is they who make them acquainted with the Gospel. In short, there is no greater or nobler authority on Earth than that of parents over their children.*" He added that the diligent rearing of children was the greatest service to the world, both temporally and spiritually, both for life today and for posterity. Marry someone who shares your values because it's teamwork to raise kids.

I suppose you could say I got lucky when I married your mother. More to the point, I was blessed by God. Mom was a Godly and attractive young woman. She had an impeccable reputation in our church, was a good student in college, and was considered a spiritual woman. She mentored other people. On Sundays after church, she spent time going to a convalescent hospital where she ministered to the elderly. She didn't have to do this. There were no college credits to be gained. She did it on her own, wanting to be a blessing to others. As one who was committed to God, I found myself drawn to her.

I recognized that I could build a family with your mother. I wouldn't have to worry about other men in her life. I knew I was on solid ground with her.

The downside for your mother was that I was still the wild beast of a man when we first got married. Our first few years were difficult. I came from one end of the spectrum, and she came from the other. The good news is that God had gotten a hold of my life, and I had a pastor in my life who mentored me and helped to nurture and ground me.

Today, your mother remains that same good woman I married. She has mentored women in prison, served at your schools over the years, prayed for you, taken meals to friends from church who were in need, and taught a women's Bible study.

Your mother and I have the same ability to communicate with each other as ever. We can drive for four or five hours somewhere and talk the whole time. We talk about family, faith, politics, friends, and more, and we haven't gotten bored with each other yet. Communication, I have found, is one of the keys to a successful marriage.

Marriage is a divine mystery, the channel of God's sanctified grace. Marriage is truly a blessing, a gift - one of the greatest works of God. *"There is no higher office, estate, condition and work (next to the Gospel which concerns*

God Himself) than the estate of marriage," wrote Luther in "To the Knights of the Teutonic Order."

I'm not an expert on marriage, but I do know human nature. One thing I know is that you and your wife will need to have mutual respect for each other. If you don't, the marriage won't work. If you think you are better than her, you will browbeat her. If you're wimpy, she won't respect you, and both of you will be unhappy. If one or both of you are impure, there will be doubt and distrust in your marriage. And if one party dominates over the other, things won't go well. Mutual respect and admiration are essential for a marriage.

It blesses me when I call your mother and she answers the phone by saying, "Morrell," always in a positive way. She likes me, and I like her. But neither of us is timid to hold back our opinions. We face our problems, and we don't agree on everything in life. But we always have a tremendous amount of respect for each other.

A good marriage is one of the sweetest pleasures and richest rewards a human being can have. As Luther is quoted in the collection *Table Talk,* "*There is no more lovely, friendly and charming relationship or company than a good marriage.*"

A good marriage is characterized by selflessness. You should not only look for an unselfish spouse to marry but also learn to be selfless in your own life. We men are made up of 1 percent water and 99 percent ego, so keep that ego in check.

I could see right away in our marriage that selflessness is indispensable. One day we went to our tax accountant to get our taxes prepared. I was hoping to get $800 back as a refund because I wanted the money to begin to build a nest egg. Smart thing. Then we found out that we were getting back $1,200. As we were driving home, your mother said she would like to use $300 of that $1,200 to buy a new couch. I said, "*No, we are going to put that money in the bank.*" She said, "*No, I'm going to take $300, and you* *can put $900 in the bank."* One word led to another, and we had ourselves a full-blown argument.

I got home, put on my running shoes, and went out for a run. As I left the house, I slammed the door. A few miles into my run, that still, small voice spoke to my mind and said, *"That wasn't a very nice way to treat your wife. Remember, you were only hoping to get $800 back. Now you're getting back $400 more. And just as you want to provide a nest egg, your wife wants to provide a nice house, a comfortable setting."* And that small voice said, *"Give her $500. That means you're still going to have $700 to put into the bank, and she'll be happy."*

When I got home, I said, *"Joanie, I need to speak with you."* She said, *"No, I need to speak with you."* She went first. She said that the still, small voice spoke to her and said that her father had never been a person to save. He always spent everything he got. So she said, *"I'm just going to trust you that you want to provide and protect our family."*

Then I explained to your mother the conclusion I had come to. She was happy with that because she came out $200 ahead, but I was happy too. I knew deep down in my heart that out of $800, I should have given her something. But we still put $700 in the bank.

What an advantage it is when two people are unselfish and are willing to put God ahead. We have had a lot of give and take throughout our marriage. Others dig their heels in, and little things become big things. Walls build up over the years until they finally break and crumble, and there's no repairing such a marriage. At the center of the movement of marriage there needs to be God, the One to Whom we yield because He knows what is best. He knows how we function. He knows what works the most. He's the Creator, the One who designed us. He knows our egos as well as our strengths and weaknesses.

Ecclesiastes 4:9–12 (NASB) says this:

Two are better than one because they have a good return for their labor; for if either of them falls down, the one will lift up his companion. But woe to the one who falls when there is not another to lift him up! Furthermore, if two lie down together, they keep warm, but how can one be warm alone? And if one can overpower him who is alone, two can resist him. A cord of three strands is not quickly torn apart.

Remember, the third strand is the Lord, right in the middle. Good words to live by because a cord of three strands cannot be broken. It's tough. God is the one who ties it all together and keeps it together. He is for us, not against us. He wants the best, and He knows the strategy and tactics that are required for a good, solid marriage and family.

Getting back to my story, the moral is this: $500 is cheaper than divorce in the long run. After that incident, I began to understand more about what it means to be selfless. Even though I still have selfishness in me, I know that when I work through issues and remember the cord of three, things can work out. Learning to give and take is good for us. It is reasonable. It teaches us that we are not the center of the universe.

As the pastor at our wedding said, *"Two unselfish people will never get a divorce."*

Sadly, divorce has grown at epidemic proportions in America. Could it be that this has come about as the result of unrestrained selfishness among men and women in our time?

In the 1960s, then-California Governor Edmund Brown formed a commission to address California's high divorce rate. The result was the Family Court, which was designed to help marriages reconcile. Regrettably, a few short years later, California abruptly ended that practice. The court supposedly became too expensive to operate. Then, a few years later came the Family Law Act in the California Legislature, known as the "No-Fault Divorce" law.[17] The basic premise of the law was that it was "only natural that if one of the spouses is dissatisfied, he or she may demand a divorce."

Every marriage has its dissatisfactions. But to think that we can walk away and split up a marriage and family that easy is to America's detriment.

Five short years after that Family Law Act bill, forty other states had passed the same kind of no-fault divorce laws.

But God's Word is clear. As God says in Malachi 2:6 (NASB), *"I hate divorce."* Divorce is morally wrong.

Recall the earlier mention that monetary disputes are a top cause of divorce in America. When you are dating, take note of how that person handles their finances. Scripture has over 2,000 references to finances. The way we handle it shows the level of our maturity as well as our faith and trust in God.

We will decline as a society until the family stays together. Renowned pastor and broadcaster Dr. Tony Evans once said at a Promise Keepers forum that America needs healing, but before we can heal America, we have to heal the people in each state.[27] And before we heal the people in each state, we need to heal the people in each county. And before we can do that, each city needs to be healed. And within each community, each home and family must be healed. How can this happen? By the father staying in the home with his wife, committing to his family, for better or worse, and pledging to nurture, protect, and provide for his children. When the family is healed, the community will be healed. When the community is healed, so will the city, county, state, and Nation.

In addition, according to a 2000 Heritage Foundation report by Patrick Fagan and Robert Rector entitled "The Effects of Divorce on America," *"Children whose parents are divorced are increasingly the victims of abuse. They exhibit more health, behavioral and emotional problems, are involved more frequently in crime and drug abuse, and have higher rates of suicide."* [16] Children of divorced parents perform more poorly in reading, spelling, and math, and they are more likely to drop out of high school and have lower rates of college education. Furthermore, divorced families split up their income, resulting in higher rates of poverty, according to the report.

Then there are the consequences of divorce for the divorcees themselves. Scientists Richards, Hardy, and Wadsworth have studied the effects of divorce on mental health and have found the two "associate with increased anxiety and depression, and increased risk of alcohol abuse."[35] Divorce splits the assets and the heart.

In other words, if you want to be happy, healthy, and prosperous: get married once and stay married. If you want good children: get married once and stay married.

God can bless second marriages and third marriages, but more often than not, these marriages are filled with heartache. A young Christian woman in my office was in a marriage years ago, and her husband left her. She's perhaps one of the most honest, spiritual, and Godly women I know. When her husband left, instead of trying to find a man, she just prayed. She prayed, fasted, and cried every day for nine months. When she couldn't cry anymore, she would pray and fast again. Eventually, eight years later, she met a great guy who is a friend of ours to this day. They are a wonderful couple to have fun with. She once told me that her family was doing well as a blended family. But she added, "You know, it's just not God's design."

I'll forever retain a moment of wisdom that Michael Reagan shared with me over a decade ago about his father's advice. The words were simple, enough to count on one hand, but had the grip to make that one hand a strong and dependable fist to hold together an undying truth to every marriage: "Never make your wife jealous," he relayed to me. But these were words that President Ronald Reagan inevitably would share with the entire world upon the publishing of his many letters, one of which was famed for his golden guidance to his son when the latter was a groom.[34] In the letter, President Reagan wrote that:

If you truly love a girl, you shouldn't ever want her to feel, when she sees you greet . . . a girl you both know, that humiliation of wondering if she was someone who caused you to be late coming home, nor should you want any other woman to be able to meet your wife and know she was smiling behind her eyes as she looked at her, the woman you love, remembering this was the woman you rejected even momentarily for her favors.

In particular, I would stress to stay away from adultery. One way to do that is to stay away from flirtation and putting yourself in precarious situations. As 1 Thessalonians 5:22 (KJV) says, *"Abstain from all appearance of evil."* Don't even go out to lunch with a woman unless other people are with you.

Adultery gives your wife grounds for divorce, and she probably won't forgive you. Even if she somehow forgives, she won't forget. Once you break trust, it's like breaking a fine piece of china. You may be able to glue it back together, but you'll still see the cracks and flaws in it.

Adultery creates havoc in a relationship. It not only breaks trust with the spouse, but it also creates distrust in the relationship with children. It harms your credibility to advise your children in their future dating and marital relationships.

Heed the words of Proverbs 5:

My son, pay attention to my wisdom, turn your ear to my words of insight, that you maintain discretion, and your lips may preserve knowledge. For the lips of an adulteress drip honey, and her speech is smoother than oil. But in the end she is bitter as gall, sharp as a two-edged sword. Her feet go down to death; her steps lead straight to the grave. She gives no thought to the way of life; her paths wander aimlessly, but she does not know it.

Now then, my sons, listen to me; do not turn aside from what I say. Keep to a path far from her; do not go near the door of her house, lest you lose your honor to others and your dignity to one who is cruel, lest strangers feast on your wealth and your toil enrich the house of another. At the end of your life, you will groan, when your flesh and body are spent. You will say, 'How I hated discipline! How my heart spurned correction! I would not obey my teachers or turn my ear to my instructors. And I was soon in serious trouble in the Assembly of God's people.

Drink water from your own cistern, running water from your own well. Should your springs overflow in the streets, your streams of water in the public squares? Let them be yours alone, never to be shared with strangers. May your fountain be blessed and may you rejoice in the wife of your youth . . .

Why be captivated, my son, by another man's wife? Why embrace the bosom of a wayward woman? For your ways are in full view of the Lord, and he examines all your paths. The evil deeds of the wicked ensnare them; the cords of their sins hold them fast. For lack of discipline they will die, led astray by their own great folly.

Life is cruel, and so is the home-wrecking woman. What's worse: her husband may seek revenge against on you. Your flesh will be spent. Immorality will cause you to age. So will child support and alimony. And in the end, a man comes to ruin financially, physically, and spiritually in front of his friends, family, fellow churchgoers, and coworkers.

So drink water from your own well. Let your wife be the source of your pleasure as water refreshes a thirsty man. Stay with your wife and be faithful to her. Avoid immorality, including pornography. Maintain your purity. Psalm 119:9 tells us that a young man keeps his way pure *"by living according to Your Word."* Stay close to God's Word. Keep it at the center of your marriage. Read and obey.

Staying married is important to your well-being, to that of your wife, your children, your community, your state, and your country. A good marriage is a stabilizing influence for the nation.

Love,
Dad

Key Takeaways

1. *Shared values*

2. *Mutual respect and open communication*

3. *Selflessness*

V.

A FATHER'S DUTY

· · · · · ·

Dear Children,

WHAT IS A father's highest aim when raising his sons and daughters? I am reminded of the warning in Hosea 4:6: *"My people are destroyed from lack of knowledge. Because you have rejected knowledge, I also have rejected you as My priests; because you have ignored the law of your God, I also will ignore your children."*

These prophetic words were an indictment against the priests of Israel, the men called to shepherd the people in their need for religious instruction. Just as this leader had responsibility to impart the truth, so he faced condemnation when he failed in his duty. This principle holds true yesterday, today, and always. Transforming young minds and ordering young souls toward the good is our mission and holy calling. We cannot afford to err.

So far, two of you have been called to the role of parenthood. Priest of your household and guardian of God's law, you will be responsible to see your family flourish in the religious and educational spheres. As your father, I had the privilege to perform this duty, albeit with limited knowledge and many mistakes. I have always desired to see you thrive in the pursuit of true knowledge, and now, more than ever, I do not take education lightly.

When your mother and I married, she desired to be in the home and focus her entire livelihood on her family. But her job allowed us to live on two incomes, and life was good. Those first few years, I would leave work in the early afternoon, watch a little television, and work out. I knew she wanted to stay home, but I was more concerned about our financial stability. I didn't want all the pressure to rest on my shoulders.

Our church leadership stood behind Mom's desire; they recognized then what I understood later. She was a cum laude university graduate with the right priorities. The promise of a successful career could not shake her sights from a higher order of things. She wanted to raise her children well, supporting and nurturing them wholeheartedly. There is a rare beauty exuded by someone like that.

Eventually, Mom let her job go, and we began adding children to our household, all expenses entailed. Self-centered tendencies aside, I now had to provide on one paycheck. I felt fearful and utterly insufficient. This was a tough time for me and also the best thing I could have experienced. I was stretched. I grew, and I learned a hard work ethic. Most importantly, I was forced to my knees in prayer. I could choose to worry and count the cost of paying bills, building a retirement, and enrolling my children in a Christian school. But I finally committed all of this to the Lord, and I made you my undisputed priority.

I took on the full pressures of providing for my family. I saved more, spent less, and tithed consistently. I matured in many ways. Looking back, the benefits to you far outweighed any of the material costs. Mom and I have few regrets and a storehouse of great memories. Our path has been marked by wonderful milestones, and these have led our children to places far better than any we could have possibly imagined.

The one who benefited the most from this training in manhood was me. I grew in faith more than I can explain, and I was blessed more than I ever deserve. I learned that my job as a father was simply to ask, *"Lord, how do you want me to educate these children? You've entrusted them to me for only a short time. How can I commit our money to their development?"* The world, of course, would caution: *"Take."* God, in His mercy, answers: *"Give."* When He guides us to give, He is faithful and trustworthy to provide in more ways than one. I found comfort knowing that Someone greater helped me to carry the load. Year after year, He met our needs, and He exceeded our expectations as well.

As my faith was strengthened, so was my marriage. Had I ignored your mother's desire to stay home with our children, there's a good chance she would have resented me. As it turned out, she helped me carry the load by praying for me, encouraging me, and eventually running the bookkeeping business for a property management company from our home. She knew when to push her unmotivated husband out the door. Later, when I had the work ethic down, she made sure I replaced my excuses for late nights at the office with better efficiency and tighter scheduling. I was expected to be there for your games and every one of your parent-teacher conferences. Mom firmly believed in a strong presence from two parents.

Your mother deserves the praise of Proverbs 31:29: *"Many daughters have done noble things, but you surpass them all."* It's not easy to manage a family and run a household successfully. Between serving, purchasing, and planning, she was there to bandage wounds and get broken bones to the hospital after tree and skateboard incidents. She was the team mom driving you to soccer, baseball, and basketball, working in your classrooms, helping you with homework, and giving sound advice and counsel. With intelligence, perseverance, compassion, and love, she created the value in our home that makes life worth living. I couldn't have asked for a better woman to be the mother of my children.

If you want to raise your children in the fear of the Lord, find a Godly spouse. If your spouse has noble character and shares your goals, then they will daily roll up their sleeves with the boldness and courage of a soldier, managing your little tyrants without getting steamrolled. Remember that no one will love or nurture your children more than a mother—not a babysitter, not a neighbor or aunt, and not a daycare center.

To my sons: cherish your wife as the treasure she is. As Lincoln said, *"No one is poor who has a Godly mother."*

I remember early on in our marriage when your mother and I imagined the possibility of becoming wealthy. Which exotic places and fascinating friends would color our travels? We would dream about the perfect vacation home, perhaps in the mountains overlooking a lake. But we came to realize that a mansion would mean nothing if we failed our children. There would be no enjoying the fruits of our labor, only heartache if you were not walking in the truth. Knowing all of life's pitfalls, your mother and I desired then to educate you in the proper way. In the mission of discipleship, I was determined not to fail.

Parenting is a full-time job. Children are the legacy we leave to this world, so we must not become apathetic or lose focus with our material possessions. I've seen too many people over the years let their boat payments or excessive credit card debt stand in the way of what's best for their family. The question is always one of priorities. You will have to sacrifice some of your desires, but your children are worth it.

I greatly admire our daughter, Kristen, for the choices she has made in her life. Kristen had a chance at a great career, and she chose to stay home with her kids. She was an adjunct professor at Arizona Christian University in political philosophy, and she chose the same path her mother did and wanted to invest her time in homeschooling her kids.

Your mother and I were truly blessed to see our children grow in the fear of the Lord. Yet, many were the times that we stood by to console when friends walked through trials and wept over their children. Now, you know me and my faults, and I know that you sin. Despite your best efforts, your children will not be immune to traps or temptations. There may be roadblocks in your life that only God is able to overcome. Trust that He will overcome. He will hear your prayers, and He is mighty to redeem.

Be alert. Time is passing quickly. Stay in tune with your Creator, and align yourself with His priorities. Then your family will stand firm when trials come and storms rage. Put God's glory first, and your family next, and you will not fail.

Love,
Dad

KEY TAKEAWAYS

1. *Put God and the Scriptures first and your family next.*

2. *Honor and cherish the wife of your youth.*

VI.

FORMING THE CHARACTER OF OUR CHILDREN

· · · · ·

Dear Children,

TO RAISE A child, the three pillars of learning—home, church, and school—must fulfill their purposes. The home is the cornerstone, for fathers and mothers have always been the first gatekeepers of education. Before you have families of your own, ponder your duty to direct and mold your sons and daughters into right-thinking, high-minded adults. As we discuss problems surrounding the church and school, remember that the first responsibility always falls on parents. We must not relinquish this duty to anyone else.

We are told that a child born today has a life expectancy of about seventy-seven years[29]. Yet there are only a few short years to determine the shape and quality of the lifetime. Undoubtedly, the average child will receive much more education from the world about secularism than about religion. Consider what bombards a young person within their very home, from television to internet and social media to books. Such is the delight of the elder demon, Wormwood, in C. S. Lewis's *Screwtape Letters*: "*Your man has been accustomed ever since he was a boy to have a dozen incompatible philosophies dancing about together in his head."* [26] Parents alone can tip the scales.

The early American legal scholar James Kent said in a lecture titled "Of Parent and Child," *"The wants and weaknesses of children render it necessary that some person maintains them, and the voice of nature has pointed out the parent as the most fit and proper person."* There is a physical dimension to want and weakness, but there is also a spiritual dimension. Children need spiritual protection, nurture, and training. Natural affections in a child's heart make parents best suited for this job. Who else is better equipped to provide a true education, intertwining the material with the spiritual, teaching ultimate truth, goodness, and beauty? Parents have the tremendous duty to place their children on the pathway that leads to God. Only then can we teach our children to seek truth in a world that increasingly denies it.

Not enough Christian parents take their spiritual responsibilities towards their children seriously. Consider the experience of many children growing up in Christian homes. It includes a Sunday church service or youth group, with an hour and a half of praying, singing, and listening to a sermon. Add thirty seconds of prayer before dinner, and you have the full measure of a young person's spiritual diet.

In our fast-paced, low-attention-span culture, moral training from parents and religious training from the pulpit are precious commodities. The principle of reaping and sowing plays out here.

Never underestimate the power that your example can have for your children. We are called to be Christlike, and adults can imitate Christ by drawing the line between right and wrong, in turn allowing our children to imitate us.

But we must be active in our teaching of God's Word. If we desire to teach our children discernment, we must guide them into a thorough knowledge of Scripture. When they can say with the psalmist, *"I have hidden Your Word in my heart . . ."* (Ps. 119:11), then they will be ready to apply truth in the face of temptation, depression, and doubts. They will have the tools to discern the best choice of friends. They will know the joys of walking with God. It is the obligation of the father, with the help of the mother, church leaders, and teachers, to see a young person grow spiritually and become sanctified in the fruit of the Spirit. A painstaking education, overshadowed by divine grace, will allow our children to live out the virtues of *"love, joy, peace, forbearance, kindness, goodness, faithfulness, gentleness and self-control"* (Gal. 5:22–23).

Yet scriptural memory and an intellectual knowledge of moral absolutes will not solve the puzzle entirely. There is still a disconnect when well-trained young people fall prey to the deceptions of life. I believe the problem is in a radical, cultural shift toward self-centeredness. As a result of this, too many Christians hold a conflicted view of the world. They hold very loosely to Christian ideas or traditions but have learned either within or outside the home that "it's all about me." They go to church and decide their own truth. They go to church and cheat and gamble. They go to church and have abortions and divorces. In the end, they go to church and do whatever pleases them because they have learned that the world centers around them.

It is imperative, then, that we integrate the religious and intellectual, or our children will never practice what they hear preached. This integration of mind and soul can only be done effectively in the home and backed up by the work of the parents. Parents in the church must reclaim their responsibility and, most importantly, understand what's at stake.

Imagine the effects of parents and church bodies acting intentionally, setting clear goals to instill young people with conscience, which consists of the *"moral power and faculties, by which we are able to discern the difference between right and wrong, truth and falsehood, good and evil,"* to quote from early American Pastor Samuel West, in his 1776 sermon, "On the Right to Rebel Against Governors." Such intentional actions by parents and churches would leave a lasting and positive impact on the lives and souls of our young people.

In 1795, Pastor Peres Fobes preached "An Election Sermon" to his congregation at the First Congregational Church of Raynham, Massachusetts, and he said these words, which are more appropriate now than ever before,

> *By a law of nature, we all begin to exist in a state of helpless infancy, under the entire control and direction of parents. By this means children early become members of a family, which is itself an empire in miniature. Having formed in the molding age of life, proper ideas and habits of government, they become at length prepared for civil society, in larger communities. While this benevolent law of nature announces government coeval with our existence, it speaks louder than the tongue of men or of angels, the necessity of early education. Her voice to legislatures is, "depend not on the number of your laws or the severity of your fines and punishments; but lay the axe at the root of vice, take possession of the heart, and charm, if possible, the young stranger to the love of virtue and country, in the tenderest period of life. Do this, by giving birth and energy to every possible institution for the education of youth." It teaches parents also, the ministers of religion and others, that while employed in the humble office of instructing youth, their services may be as patriotic, and perhaps more useful to their country, than the wisdom of their counsels in the Senate, or the valor of their arms in the field.*

Imparting a good education is a slow and difficult process; it takes serious interest, and it takes time. Stay committed, however, and you will find yourself surrounded by those of like mind. Meanwhile, your family - *"an empire in miniature,"* as Fobes called it - will learn the habits of the government so necessary for civil society, and you, as a parent, will have performed a service more useful to your country "than the wisdom of their counsels in the Senate, or the valour of their arms in the field."

A classical Christian education aims for wholeness, for in Christianity, a supernatural Creator has infused the natural world with transcendent truth and divine love. Beauty exists because there is order in our art, music, numbers, and words. The great books and great epochs of history confirm this idea, teaching that human beauty is an ordered soul, not modern manners.

Our Founding Fathers understood the far-reaching effects of a classical education built on great books.

The skills of public speaking, and that nearly lost art of reading aloud, are acquired around the dining room table. As parents guide, correct, and discuss, a child learns to research or accumulate facts, reason or discern underlying patterns and principles, and relate this wisdom to a greater body of knowledge. These reasoning skills are essential, whether a child grows to become a businessperson, scientist, historian, or member of Congress.

Education is more than learning dates and names, for these are incidental to true learning. As John Ruskin wrote, *"Education does not mean teaching people to know what they do not know. It means teaching them to behave as they do not behave."* Do we teach our children to apply themselves and study, to listen and discern, to be quiet and ponder? These are the human behaviors that lead to a lifetime of learning, as with the men and women of Proverbs 18:15: *"The heart of the discerning acquires knowledge, but the ears of the wise seek it out."*

The scriptural command to *"Train up a child in the way he should go"* from Proverbs 22:6 (KJV) is a duty to instruct the young in the statutes of God when you sit in your house and when you walk along the road. This is why I recommend homeschooling your children. *"Teach them to your children, talking about them when you sit at home and when you walk along the road, when you lie down and when you get up. Write them on the doorframes of your houses and on your gates . . ."* (Deut. 6:7-9).

However, thirty years ago we chose Christian schools, which were much better then. We developed a hybrid model where we sent you to a

Christian school but were compelled to keep a close eye and stay involved in what you were being taught.

We carefully chose the schools that would furnish you with knowledge, and we thank God for the choices we had. No school is invariably perfect, and we did experience occasional problems. We always succeeded in resolving these issues, however, because we made it our rule to deal in civility and respect. We never wanted to alienate teachers or burn bridges with the staff. Rather, we constantly strove to help the school become better.

The schools you choose should view themselves as educational "subcontractors" in a clear partnership with the parents. The primary obligation to instruct and develop children lies with the parents. It is not the school's responsibility to guarantee that your high school graduate is properly educated. Your children may need a tutor from time to time, not to mention regular discussion and encouragement at home. Don't drop the ball there. And find a school that will reinforce the moral principles you teach at home. See that the curriculum is dedicated to truth, and the educators are committed to the fear of God as the beginning of wisdom. Then your student will build a solid foundation for a virtuous life.

In the end, now that you are out of high school and college, choosing what we did has proven to be a good decision. It was good that your mother was there for you all—to bandage your wounds and drive you to the hospital as you broke bones and fell out of trees. When you, David, got stuck in a rabbit cage and could not get your head out, she was there for you. She was also there to help you do your homework and drive you to soccer, baseball, and basketball games. Mom participated as a team mom of milestones in your and her lives and memories for all of us—in those things that make life worth living.

Lastly, I close with these thoughts from our great American heritage. James Wilson, a Founding Father of our country, said in his "Lectures on Law" in 1791, *It is the duty of parents to maintain their children decently, and according to their circumstances; to protect them according to the dictates of prudence, and to educate them in according to the suggestions of a judicious and zealous regard for their usefulness, their respectability and their happiness."*

I have full confidence in your abilities and love to do the right thing.

Love,
Dad

Key Takeaways

1. *Parents are to be the role models for their children.*

2. *Parents have the responsibility to be the guardians of their children's mind and soul.*

VII.

THE ABOLITION OF EDUCATION

· · · · · ·

Dear Children,

WHAT IS THE highest good a father can do when educating his sons and daughters? For this question, I'd like to bring back verse 6 from Hosea 4 for a second look: *"My people are destroyed from lack of knowledge. Because you have rejected knowledge, I also have rejected you as My priests. Because you have ignored the law of your God, I also will ignore your children."*

These words offer to us the strong warning that we ought not take lightly education and the pursuit of knowledge. Each of us should spend time transforming our mind and ordering our soul toward the good. That is why I will go on about the subject of education at length. I hope that through this, you will see the necessity of a good education.

As we discussed Chapter 5, this verse from Hosea is an indictment against the priests of Israel whose duty was not only to be guardians of God's laws but also to help God's people flourish in religious instruction. And just as these priests had a job and were condemned for not fulfilling it, so it will be your job as a father, the priest of your household, to be the guardian of God's laws and help your family flourish. In both the religious and educational contexts, it is imperative that you integrate the spiritual and the intellectual together. As Dr. Thomas J. Burke, professor of philosophy and religion, said, *"But in order to fulfill his place in the cosmos, man must know who he is and what he must do to fulfill his destiny. To live as he ought, he must understand his God, his world and himself and this requires a broad grounding in all those arts and sciences that address Him qua human being."*[9] It is necessary, then, that before we act and live, we must know. Living begins with learning.

While learning is often seen as a thing for children and young adults, aged six years to twenty-two, it is, in fact, an endeavor that consumes a lifetime and is, at the end, never completed. For as you grow in knowledge, you become more keenly aware of how much there is that you do not know. What should grow within you is not arrogance springing from what you know but humility and wonder at the world and how much of it you will never understand. A mark of a good education is not haughtiness but modesty, not pride but humility. In many ways, the chief fruit of a worthy education is your own awareness of your ignorance. This is why Socrates defines the wise person as *he who knows that he does not know.* I have learned to be skeptical of anyone who believes education can ever be completed or anyone who acts as though they have the world figured out. The universe is much too complex and wonderful and beautiful for any mortal to sum up within a lifetime, much less a few years of education.

As I have experienced God, I have come to understand the great importance of knowledge.

In his book, *The Abolition of Man,* C. S. Lewis reminds us:

> *"In the Republic, the well-nurtured youth is one 'who would see most clearly whatever was amiss in ill-made works of man or ill-grown works of nature, and with a just distaste would blame and hate the ugly even from his earliest years and would give delighted praise to beauty, receiving it into his soul and being nourished by it, so that he becomes a man of gentle heart'."*[25]

It is becoming harder to find adults today who are well-nurtured, who see clearly what is amiss in society, and who hate ugliness and love beauty and truth. Few have nourished their souls and hearts in order to do these. It is the mark of either no education or a bad one.

When David was a teenager, I took him to visit various college campuses throughout the country. We took a number of tours with other parents, and I was able to observe what parents asked. *"Is this school safe?"* Good question. Another: *"Is the food good?" "Is there enough parking?" "What is the area like?" "What are the dorms like?" "Is there drinking on campus?" "Will they get the college 'experience'?"* All of these questions are fine, but they concern only a student's physical needs. We also have a soul. I do not recall ever hearing questions like, *"Will my student learn to be a successful human being?" "How will their souls be nourished?" "Will they know truth and beauty?" "Will they learn to serve the highest good?"* If you believe we are only physical beings, then it makes sense that these questions are not asked. But if we are more than physical beings, spiritual beings, our questions should reflect this fact. Every parent should know that we are spiritual beings and that there are things in life more valuable than money and careers. Sadly, today, education is seen as merely job preparation and certification. But what is the good of money—a means—if one does not know the end: how are we to live?

A Founding Father, Gouverneur Morris, once said that education was the *"effect of society on the habits and principles of each individual, forming him at an early period of life to act afterwards the part of a good citizen and contribute in his turn to the formation of others. Hence, it results that the progress towards freedom must be slow"* (quoted in Thomas G. West's *Vindicating the Founders: Race, Sex, Class, and Justice in the Origins of America*).[44]

A good education will impart not only knowledge but also wisdom, prudence, and humility as well. It will help young men and women to understand their place below God and their duty to their fellow human beings. A father's prayer should be for his children to become intellectually well-formed and successful and, more importantly, to know the good.

In 1804, Rev. Samuel Kendall of Weston, Massachusetts, delivered a sermon titled "Religion, the Only Sure Basis of Free Governments," stressing the importance of education:

> *If we depart from the principles of our ancestors, neglect religion and its institutions, are not attentive to the instruction of our youth in religious and moral duty, as well as in human literature, indulge a spirit of innovation, are indifferent to the moral character of rulers, and yield to the temptations to luxury and dissoluteness of manners, which increasing wealth presents, we shall soon find ourselves unable to support the constitutions which have been the pride of our Nation, and the admiration of the world. But if we diligently attend to all these things, set our own hearts unto all the words of the divine law,* **and command our children to observe and do them, it will be our life, and we shall prolong our days in this good land. The mouth of the Lord hath spoken it** (emphasis mine).*

Our leaders, over two hundred years ago, understood this more than those who lead now.

Today, as the world progresses in things like business, transportation, and technology—which are, by the way, all fine things—we assume that morality should be in lock-step with these advancements. However, because human nature is what it is—unchanging, flawed, and prone to evil—this is not the case. This is why when we progress materially, we must occupy ourselves ever more earnestly in education to guide ourselves through a chaotic world. We must learn how to wield the newfound benefits of science, for the progress of science can either provide innumerable benefits to the world or immortal horrors when men use them wrongly. This is why it is so dangerous that moral instruction has been divorced from modern education, that places (in the hands of its subjects) a power unknown to all of human civilization. As we leave truth behind and abandon its sisters, beauty, and goodness, we no longer know how to use this power. It is not too late, however. We can still learn.

I pose these problems to you in order that you might consider these things before you have your own families, when you will have the duty to mold your sons and daughters into well-thinking, high-minded adults.

There is a right way to pursue an education, and that is to try always to become more Christlike, ceaselessly developing a conscience, teaching others to do the same, and learning to distinguish between right and wrong. You will want your children to know the joys of walking with God and understanding the consequences that come by walking outside of God's umbrella of protection.

It has been my goal to instill in you a conscience, so that if you do ever walk away from faith, you will recognize the wrong you've done and will not find any justification for your behavior. I hope that peace will not be present in your soul until you return to the Lord. But how much sadder it would be for me to see one of you commit adultery, embezzle money, abuse alcohol, and then tell me that you are walking in Christ or not under the law. There seems to be a disconnect today within the church. It is our obligation to make an effort to grow spiritually and move forward. The mark of a Christian is to develop, to become sanctified. As Galatians 5:22–23 says, *"but the fruits of the spirit are the virtues of love, joy, peace, patience, kindness, goodness, faithfulness, gentleness, and self-control."* These all begin with grace, are developed through education, and are completed again by grace. What parents can do in this process is provide support and education inside and outside of the home. For if the fruits of the Spirit are absent, there is reason for grave concern…and potential for tragedy.

If you become a parent and find yourself having failed, do not fret, for there is power in prayer. God cares, and He can redeem things. He is the God of second, third, and fourth chances. But do not think that if public school does not work out, you can pray later, and God will make it right.

That is not always the case. That is like a Hail Mary pass in a football game when you are fourth and ten with two seconds to go. It usually does not succeed. The goal is to be in the lead in the last two seconds of the game. Likewise, the goal is to prepare, prepare, prepare.

We, as parents, must take the initiative and impart the Word of God into young children's hearts and minds. Many good parents who serve God faithfully year after year have kids who seem to be doing poorly on the spiritual and moral side of the equation. How does this happen? Why the disconnect? As I have studied and searched for an answer to this question, I have found some. I have noticed that there are many pieces to the puzzle, each of which play an important part in the puzzle. Among these pieces are quality of friends, society's ills, free will, original sin, television, radicalism, liberalism, or a lack of moral and religious training from the parents as well as from the pulpit. And the list goes on. Still, a number of our friends I have seen have been aware of these pitfalls, yet somehow still raised children who have sadly fallen prey to the deceptive thinking of this world. Despite all the roadblocks life brings, God is always able to overcome. And in His divine plan, He has provided a way for us to overcome many of these obstacles. And the principal weapon God has given children are parents, the guardians of their souls. We, as parents, must make wise decisions in the molding of our children's hearts, minds, and souls. Though this takes work, it is our duty.

In the 1800s, Thomas Jefferson commissioned a study designed to gain insight into America's greatness and answer the question: how did America so quickly rise to prominence throughout the world? Mr. DuPont, who led the study, concluded that our greatness had much to do with what happened in the home in terms of education. This is what he wrote,

Most young Americans, therefore, can read, write and cipher. No more than four in a thousand are unable to write legibly, even neatly. . . . In America, a great number of people read the Bible and all the people read a

newspaper. The fathers read aloud to their young children while breakfast is being prepared, a task which occupies the mother for three-quarters of an hour each morning. And as the newspapers of the United States are filled with all sorts of narratives, commentaries on matters of political, physical, philosophic information, information on agriculture, the arts, travel, navigation and also extracts from all the best books in America and Europe, they disseminate an enormous amount of information, something which is helpful to the young people especially when they arrive at an early age, where the father resigns his place as reader and favors the older child who can best succeed him. It is because of this education we Americans have more great men than any other nation in history. We have the advantage of having a large portion of moderately well-informed men although their education may seem less perfect, it is nevertheless better and more equally distributed but this does not mean that education cannot be improved. [14]

In addition, we must teach our offspring the Scriptures. For a true education is incomplete without the ultimate truth, the goodness, and beauty. If you do not seek God, you will soon find that truth will be just as elusive. But if you seek God, you will find truth. And when we are serious about seeking truth, we will find truth, which always leads to God. This is a double benefit.

Therefore, we, as parents, must provide a good education and teach our children to be truth seekers in a world that increasingly denies the very existence of it.

There is a reason, though, that has made this subject nearer and dearer to me. I mentioned in Chapter 5 the considerations I shared with your mother, earlier in life, about what we would do if we ever became wealthy; the travels with friends, the exotic destinations, the vacation homes choices and the best views to go with them. Eventually, we realized that there were more fundamental questions to ask: what if our children were not walking with the Lord? What good would all of this wealth be if our flesh and blood were rebelling against God? Could we have peace? Could we enjoy the fruits of our labor? It would break our hearts to know that our children were not walking in truth. We desire, above all, to see our children victorious in Him. This would give us peace and well-being and the ability to enjoy the fruits of our labor and to face the world with confidence.

In 2021, the OECD reports on life expectancy at birth lies in the age of high seventies—approximately between seventy-three and seventy-nine years for men and women, respectively.[31] Yet, as parents, we have only a few short years to lay the foundation for their lives, to set them on the right path. This is why Scripture tells us to *"Train up a child in the way he should go"* (Proverbs 22:6 KJV). So despite all of life's pitfalls, it has been your mother's and my responsibility—as it will be one day your responsibility—to educate our children in the proper way. Our children are disciples, a legacy we leave to the future world. So it is imperative that the decisions regarding education are made early, prayerfully, and well. For it is through parents and a proper education that children will be led to truth, to the pathway heading toward God and a solid faith.

A right education, then, starts in the home. It is only after this has been done well that the second thing can be done, that is, choosing the right school—and later, the right college. And the third pillar of a worthwhile education is choosing the right church—in short, it should be a church that is serious about teaching the truths of Scripture.

Until the foundation is built well for our children, we, as parents, must be alert and on guard to send them into the real world. They will have the rest of their lives to live in it. Why not send them out prepared and armed with those things that are necessary not only to live, but to live well?

Parents have a tremendous responsibility to educate their children well. I believe we can lose our children if we educate them poorly. And one of the most important building blocks in a true education is developing not only their intellect but also their heart and soul, which needs to happen at home. School and home must work together toward this common goal.

Some years back, I had the opportunity to be a delegate for the California State Legislature for the inauguration of President Bush's second term. One day, when we were back in Washington D. C., we toured the Library of Congress. On the ceiling, I read this quote from Shakespeare's King Henry VI: *"Ignorance is the curse of God; knowledge the wing wherewith we fly to Heaven."*

When one lacks education in the higher things, he remains ignorant. Now ignorance is not stupidity. It is the state of not knowing; it is not the state of not being able to know. The corollary, then, is that ignorance can be worked upon. One can make the effort to learn things, which is done by seeking knowledge and truth in a spirit of humility. This is what leads one out of the bondage of ignorance. And when one begins this process, he is drawn closer to God. For knowledge leads us to truth, truth guides us to God, and God brings us to Heaven. And the first step to all of this is found in Proverbs 9:10: *"The fear of the Lord is the beginning of wisdom."*

Many Christian schools, unlike public schools, work from this premise. They believe that fear of God is, in fact, the beginning of wisdom. Unfortunately, some are adopting the cultural norms we see today. Fear the Lord, and you will obtain the right kind of knowledge. You will live better and more virtuously.

Consider the following verses:

"The mind of the discerning acquires knowledge, and the ear of the wise seeks knowledge." —Proverbs 18:15

"Desire without knowledge is not good—how much more will hasty feet miss the way." —Proverbs 19:2

"When a mocker is punished, the simple gain wisdom; by paying attention to the wise they get knowledge." —Proverbs 21:11

"Apply your heart to instruction and your ears to words of knowledge."
—Proverbs 23:12

"[T]hrough knowledge its rooms are filled with rare and beautiful treasuries." —Proverbs 24:4

"A ruler with discernment and knowledge maintains order."
—Proverbs 28:2

"But just as you abound in everything, in faith and utterance and knowledge and in all earnestness and in the love we inspired in you, see that you abound in this gracious work also." —2 Corinthians 8:7 (NASB)

"And this I pray, that your love may abound still more and more in real knowledge and all discernment, so that you may approve the things that are excellent, in order to be sincere and blameless until the day of Christ."
—Philippians 1:9–10 (NASB)

"Paul, a servant of God and the apostle of Jesus Christ, to further the faith of God's elect and their knowledge of the truth that leads to Godliness—in the hope of eternal life, which God, who does not lie, promised before the beginning of time, and which now at His appointed season He has brought to light through the preaching entrusted to me by the command of God our Savior." —Titus 1:1–3

"But grow in the grace and knowledge of our Lord and Savior Jesus Christ. To Him be the glory both now and forever! Amen." —2 Peter 3:18

The goal of learning is to attain knowledge and wisdom for a happier life—a life walked according to God's plan for us. And when we do this, true success is around the corner. Knowledge is the first and necessary step to success.

Another reason for attaining knowledge is expressed in the words of author and Hillsdale College president Dr. Larry Arnn as he speaks about the benefits of sound learning in a classical education setting and why it is essential for religious freedom and liberty. In his book *Liberty and Learning: The Evolution of American Education* (2004), Dr. Arnn states, "'*Civil and religious liberty' are named as one of the two beneficiaries of 'sound learning' in the Hillsdale Articles of Association. These are also the highest principles of the Nation.*"[3]

The purposes of education, then, are not only academic but also political. This is especially vital in America, a free society governed by consent, as each person is both governed and governor. Each must practice the art of statesmanship and, above all, self-restraint. If citizens cannot govern themselves—their passions, emotions, and habits—they will not be able to preserve a free society. As Bishop George Berkeley wrote in his treatise *Siris: A Chain of Philosophical Reflections and Inquiries* (350), "*[He] that hath not much meditated upon God, the human mind, and the summum bonum [the highest good], may possibly be a thriving earthworm, but will most indubitably make a sorry patriot and a sorry statesman.*"[7]

Arnn writes, "*If a nation is to remain free, its citizens must know how to distinguish good action from bad, justice from injustice, liberty from licentiousness and freedom from tyranny.*"

And these things can be done only by good learning and good conversation. What better place to find these than in the home and school committed to teaching truth?

Unfortunately, there are few schools that offer this type of learning. In a 1798 essay entitled "Of the Mode of Education Proper in a Republic," Founding Father Benjamin Rush declared that "*the only foundation of a useful education in a republic is to be laid in Religion. Without this there can be no virtue, and without virtue there can be no liberty.*"

When our son, David, was a senior in college, he wrote an explanation of what a good liberal arts education is. It will, he wrote, *"serve the ends of living a more comfortable life and also living a good life."* He continued:

However, the search for truth ought to take precedence above the rest, for tradition and truth are not dusty corpses displayed for the stares of passing faces, or the remnants of generations long past, but rather ordered melodies lost amongst the cries of progress. A society that ignores these is like a ship that travels without a compass or any means of direction; and the beacon of hope amidst the darkened thinking of our society is for a renewal in America of faith and reason, a return to Jerusalem and Athens.

The best time to do this is in those early years. The number-one foundation for a good education starts in the home. Even having children in a Christian school does not guarantee success. Nevertheless, it is still a better choice considering the alternatives.

So create the best environment you can where your children will thrive in the early stages of their personal development and surround them with people of good character. You will have a much better shot at making them good. Likewise, surround yourself with people who are smarter than yourself, and you will become smarter. Surround yourself and your children with Godly people; you and they will become Godly. Christian schools try to instill the knowledge of God as the solution for enriching one's soul. I know a number of good parents who have had to sacrifice by working two jobs and cutting back on material things just so they could pay the tuition for their kid's education. It is money well spent. Next, and more importantly, Christian schools should be looked at as the subcontractor in partnership with the parents. The school you choose should be reinforcing what is being taught at the home. You do not want a school or teacher working against you, unraveling what you weave each day.

Remember that knowledge sets the captives free and makes for a better society. We cannot afford to have faulty reasoning. This is why we must prepare—we must prepare for the battle for the hearts and souls of Americans. We must stay close to God and be engaged and know how to win. Consider these paraphrased verses from Ephesians 5:8–13 and 15–17:

Live as children of light (for the fruit of the light consists in all goodness, righteousness and truth) and find out what pleases the Lord. Have nothing to do with the fruitless deeds of darkness, but rather expose them. It is shameful even to mention what the disobedient do in secret. But everything exposed by the light becomes visible—and everything that is illuminated becomes a light. . . . Be very careful, then, how you live—not as unwise, but as wise, making the most of every opportunity, because the days are evil. Therefore do not be foolish but understand what the Lord's will is (emphasis mine).

Likewise, look to Ephesians 6:10–18:

Finally, be strong in the Lord and His mighty power. Put on the full armor of God, so that you can take your stand against the devil's schemes. For our struggle is not against flesh and blood, but against the rulers, against the authorities, against the powers of this dark world and against the spiritual forces in the Heavenly realms. Therefore put on the full armor of God, so when the day of evil comes, you may be able to stand your ground, and after you have done everything, to stand. Stand firm then, with the belt of truth buckled around your waist, with the breastplate of righteousness in place, and with your feet fitted with the readiness that comes from the gospel of peace. In addition to all this, take up the shield of faith with which you can extinguish all the flaming arrows of the evil one. Take the helmet of salvation and the sword of the Spirit, which is the Word of God.

And pray in the Spirit on all occasions with all kinds of prayers and requests. With this in mind, be alert and always keep on praying for all the Lord's people.

Despite all the negative things I have said about public education, millions of Americans have come through the system and will continue to do so in the future. Consequently, we cannot afford to abandon the public schools. Rather, we must win and fight to get them back. So I recommend that you help change the course and direction of the public school systems in America for you and your children. Our citizens are worth it. Our liberties are at stake. Exercise your civic responsibility boldly and strategically.

But until then, send them to a private school, or homeschool them if you can. Guard them, shield them, prepare them, and send them off at the appropriate time into the world—only after you have solidified a foundation built upon the bedrock of truth. Then, and only then, will they be able to divide and conquer.

Love,
Dad

Key Takeaways

1. *Learning never ends.*

2. *The fear of the Lord is the beginning of wisdom.*

3. *A proper education begins in the home.*

VIII

WAITING FOR SUPERMAN AND THE FUTURE OF PUBLIC EDUCATION

· · · · ·

I WROTE THIS article under the title "To Fix Schools, Return to Founding Principles," published in the Riverside Press-Enterprise on August 30, 2013.

When did we accept average as ordinary? Most Americans agree that our education system is badly fractured. We read continuously about how America's and California's academic rankings are slipping at an alarming rate.

CEOs like Sky Dayton (founder of EarthLink) have warned that skills for success are often lacking in college graduates. The National Science Foundation indicates that America's inability to produce graduates in STEM programs (science, technology, engineering, and math) has forced employers to seek candidates from other countries to fill critical positions. In our mad rush to change with the times, have we forgotten how to produce a quality workforce? If so, how do we recapture the things that once made California's educational system one of the best in the world?

First, recognize that this crisis in education is both an economic and a moral problem. Human capital is the main driver for long-term economic success, which requires an educated workforce. Our economy could not survive without those who are directed by a strong moral compass.

Furthermore, problems with education also point to a crisis of freedom. History clearly teaches that a free, self-governed, and prosperous people must value liberty. If voters are unenlightened about our constitutional rights, it sends us down a dangerous path.

Many good ideas have been offered to fix the educational system. Returning decision-making power to local districts, as we took steps to do this year, will help improve the mess created by Sacramento and Washington, DC. Additionally, creative policies - like Assembly Bill 51 (a bill I jointly sponsored, which would have offered California State University students, who were entering STEM fields of study, the opportunity to earn their bachelor's degrees for $10,000) - can move us in the right direction.

But at the same time, I believe our problems require a return to basic foundational principles. Before digital classrooms and standardized tests, our great Nation produced many of the brightest minds in history. Though times change, these principles have not.

How can education produce strong minds and sturdy, honest character? University founders understood that education requires a core set of values. Their mottos included words like courage, piety, honor, duty, and liberty. But in our zeal to give students a taste of everything, we have failed to impart a hunger for the best. I believe this road, where children receive no absolutes, leads to nowhere except a drop in academic and economic advantages.

We must start with teaching our children how to think. That includes emphasizing the importance of memorizing facts that can be used in critical thinking. We must lay the groundwork for mastering effective writing and public speaking—all skills necessary for a well-rounded and prepared workforce.

Most importantly, we must also become champions of parental involvement. What early Americans knew, modern Americans are rediscovering:

a student's performance is largely the result of a parent-teacher partnership. Rev. Peres Fobes wrote in 1799 that the law of nature *"teaches parents and others that while employed in the humble office of instructing our youth, their services may be as patriotic and perhaps more useful to their country than their wisdoms aand their counsels in the Senate."*

These principles have stood the test of time and will preserve our Golden State with economic, political, and moral prosperity. Every problem of education today is an opportunity for each of us to step forward and invest in the lives of young students. If we perform this duty without fail, the next generation will become the best depository for our national safety and happiness.

IX.

CHOOSING A COLLEGE

. . . . .

"For contemplation and valor, He was formed." —Milton

Dear Children,

JUST BECAUSE A child reaches eighteen years old does not mean a father's job is done. If you have done your job well up to this point, what you have done is laid a good foundation from the time they were born to the day they graduated from high school. But now they must be educated in a way that instills virtue and rightly forms the soul. Consequently - and equally important to good parenting in the first eighteen year of a child's life – is directing them toward a good college education. But before you release your young students to professors who have an agenda and are trying to dismantle their foundation, make sure their ark is solidly built. And then when the time is right, you will know with confidence that it is time to send your child out to the world and release them to the wolves. They will have the right tools to win and not be shaken.

There are two things that can be said about many college professors: first, they are, by and large, extremely liberal; second, they are extremely interested in engineering students to think just as they do. In fact, I myself have seen a number of good people send their young, beautiful, and bright teens to colleges where all of what the parents have instilled in their children for eighteen years is quickly torn away by professors who profess a doctrine of nihilism and moral relativism. The foundations of these students are shaken and torn down and replaced with a new set of vain doctrines. Others renounce the faith they have grown up with. In fact, a number of reports and polling data suggest a common story of many Christian teens: they go to college, leave the faith, and never come back to it again.[6] Why, considering the state of today's university, would they not go off to these college campuses and come back with all sorts of flawed philosophies, gender confusion, and general spiritual malaise, among other things?

I do not advocate that we go into hiding with our children. But remember: what, according to Christ, does light have in common with darkness? Why send your young student to a college where darkness assaults the light? Why provide your children into the care of people who will tear down everything that you have spent a large part of a lifetime attempting to instill? It is important that one take great care in presenting a child into to the rest of society – good and bad, as they come – and not before they are ready. Of course, I have no problem introducing them: but this can only be rightly done when they are adequately prepared.

As I've taken time to scour various college and university websites, it becomes easier to see what is happening to higher education in America. After a brief cruise on the Internet, I found different classes being offered on some of our Nation's leading university campuses. One college had classes entitled "Managing Diversity" and "Contemporary Feminist Theory and Practice." Remember, I am practical; I believe that college is to make you smart, make you good, and prepare you for a life of service and virtue and honor. What, then, do these classes have to do in moving a student toward any of these high and noble ideals? In fact, it is difficult to find any value in classes such as these. Another college had a class on "Feminist Perspective on Art History" and another on "Comparative Ethnic Relations."

It should be no wonder that our culture is declining, and many of our students seem to lack wisdom, discernment, and spirituality.

Yale University, whose roots can be traced back to the 1640s, was granted a charter in 1701 that declared it to be a place "*Wherein youth may be instructed in the arts and sciences and through the blessings of Almighty God may be fitted for publick employment both in church and civil state.*" Today, Yale no longer advocates this. And then Harvard, whose motto declares a commitment to veritas, or truth, now seems to be a bastion for relativism and secular progressivism. This is the same college that, in 1643, justified its own existence by its purpose and mission, which was "To advance learning and perpetuate it to posterity dreading to leave an illiterate ministry to the churches."

Likewise, the founders of Harvard Divinity School insisted that "*Every encouragement be given to the serious, impartial and unbiased investigation of Christian truth.*"

A passage from a local Christian university here in Southern California speaks volumes to me about where America's educational system once was and where it is now and how disastrous is the turn that it has taken. By comparing its current mission statement with its former one, there will emerge an archetype of the direction colleges throughout America have taken. For this college is unique in neither its former mission statement, the current one, nor the fact that it has abandoned the former in favor of something new. Most college mission statements from the founding of each school, in fact, have two things in common: one, they are beautiful and contain high and noble things, and two, no one in the school now even knows what it says nor has any desire to fulfill that which it prescribes.

The mission of this same university was once insightful and right, and made this school a good place to educate your student. The mission statement from 1908, titled "The Aim," said, "*To mold the mind and the heart so that in the conflict in life, keenness and conscience shall go forth together. It seeks to impress its pupils that the idea of making men is more important than making money. It is better to live a life than to make a living.*[32] Though short, it makes a powerful argument. It is a defense of making a person good rather than making her or him rich. It is of utmost importance, it suggests, that a person become a good spouse, father or mother, employee, employer, and citizen. There is nothing in this statement that would suggest that there is anything wrong with making money, but it is absolutely true that it is not the highest thing. Of course, a good education will bring money. But it is when one has money that the question becomes even more pertinent, what am I to do with it? How am I to live? This is why an education for the soul is more important than job certification. It is of infinite importance that a man or woman became a person of integrity and possessed of a good character. For God will use men and women who have improved their souls, who are tough but have soft hearts. This is the difference between the old idea of education and today's idea that holds an education to be about job training, making money, and seeking pleasure. How I long for colleges of yesteryear.

Now let us fast forward more than one hundred years later to this university and view its mission in the modern day. Within the time elapsed, they've adjusted their statement a number of times, so my example will involve one instance observed in this past decade. The contrast will be obvious. *"[This] private, independent liberal arts university…[is] committed to providing a personalized education that frees students to make enlightened choices."*[15, 41]

They emphasize academic rigor, curricular diversity, and innovative teaching. They foster a community of scholars and encourage a pluralistic notion of values by challenging assumptions and stereotypes in both classes and activities. An education goes beyond training to embrace a reflective understanding of our world; it proceeds from information to insight, from knowledge to meaning.

Welcoming intellectually curious students of diverse religious, ethnic, national, and socioeconomic backgrounds, the university seeks to develop responsible citizenship as part of a complete education. They encourage a community atmosphere with exceptional opportunity for student leadership and interaction. For working adults, the university offers innovative academic programs at convenient locations and times.

They blend liberal arts and professional programs, applied and theoretical study, traditional majors, and self-designed contracts for graduation. Small classes enable each student to participate in class discussion, work closely with professors, and receive extensive individual attention. They remain sensitive to contemporary trends in society and challenges students to commit themselves to a lifetime of learning.

First, notice the length relative to its older mission. It has grown. It appears as though this is trying to be all things to all people. It attempts to include all in a spirit of relativism and multicultural nonsense. Second, notice the number of contemporary marketing terms, which have less meaning every time they are used. They are trite, worn out, and tired phrases. They cease, however, to convey the power that language holds when used well.

For example, they encourage students to make "enlightened choices." How nice. This, however, would require there to be a moral right and wrong—a thing whose existence they cannot admit without first abandoning "enlightened decisions" as the measure of an act.

They also emphasize "academic rigor." But, then again, should not all universities claim this? "Innovative teaching" is a phrase I do not understand. Maybe it is like the Jetsons of the future. Also, what does it mean to have a pluralistic notion of values? If I understand it correctly, that phrase means that they have different kinds of values. Does this mean that the people value all things differently? If so, what if a person does not value human life, liberty, or the dignity of other human beings? Does this mean that we should respect the actions that flow from a belief that another human being is valueless? In other words, what if a person does not value something that is inherently valuable? It seems that a pluralistic notion of values is a smokescreen for relativism, which holds that human beings define reality and may act according to the reality they have defined.

It is clear that this university has strayed excessively from its original mission – a matter which could be objectionable only in a world in which truth does not change. This strategy of appealing to everyone is weak. It is better to be true to yourself and do the right thing: indeed, this works.

These two mission statements represent a clear, contrasting distinction between the past and the present: the good and the bad. It shows clearly where the problem lies in education today. In earlier years, Americans understood the necessity of rightly forming the mind and the soul; they also understood the importance of making men and women become great thinkers. Like this university did in 1908, many American colleges once had a firm basis for teaching truth and transforming students into people of conviction, passion, and courage. This way of thinking was an integral part in our founding and in the lives of the men and women who helped to make our Nation great. Amen to this college's mission statement in 1908, but shame to this college and other universities who have now bought into this modern thinking and have changed for the sake of being contemporary rather than good.

It is a wonder to consider that so many colleges were founded under such ideals of virtue, honor, piety, freedom, righteousness, and goodness. Though it is no small thing to abandon entirely that for which a thing was founded, these colleges are a few among many that have done just that. How does this happen?

First, it happens by becoming materialistic, when we care more about the means of living than the ends toward which they aim.

Second, this phenomenon occurs when people become complacent, when they are no longer vigilant against the invasion of wrong philosophies into the hearts and minds of the students.

And finally, this happens to the schools themselves so that parents, who are often more concerned with their two-week vacation and paying their mortgage payment, can easily place their child's college education at the bottom of their list of priorities.

Vigilance and careful attention of the mind is necessary when the words like *honor* and *virtue* have become controversial and terms of offense. It is just these things, in addition to *"religion, morality, and knowledge,"* that are, according to the Northwest Ordinance of 1787, *"necessary to good government and happiness of mankind."* Christopher Flannery wrote a similar thing in an essay posted at the Ashbrook Center's website:

> *Democracy requires more of its citizens than any other form of government. It depends on the capacity of the citizens to govern themselves but the habits and dispositions of self-government are difficult to acquire and to sustain. They are rooted in moral and political philosophies in which each new generation must be educated. It is no accident that history provides so few examples of successful and enduring democracies. In the American democracy, today we have largely lost sight of those moral and political principles which provide the common ground of American political community and inform the civic character required of the American citizen.*[18]

I recall when Matthew faced in Catholic high school one teacher who was a socialist and another one an admitted communist. They denied the sanctity of human life and debunk all that is good, true, or beautiful. I am proud of Matthew for the stands he has taken. I cannot urge parents enough to be, in light of this, extremely cautious as you send a child into a climate where evil things are promoted and glorified.

Over the years, every step of the way, God has been faithful to clothe, shelter, and supply us with good things. Prayerfully, your mother and I have considered which of the many colleges would be the best, what would best instill the right principles, what school would put you on the path of truth and lead you to God. So before we cut our children loose into the world, we wanted to reason together with them and help them choose a good college. On our end of things, we did our homework in researching over one hundred colleges and visiting quite a few of them. In doing this, we learned some important things. Also, note all of our children are independent thinkers, so we didn't dictate but rather worked, visited, and reasoned through this process.

In the early 1950s, a number of American colleges were confronted with a decision the answer to which would shape the direction they would follow for the next fifty years and beyond. The question was whether or not these colleges would accept funds from the federal government. As the college leaders gathered together to decide this question, many chose to accept the funds while others, distrusting federal action in areas it does not belong, rejected the money and the ties coming with it. The latter believed that in accepting these funds, they would be unduly subjected to the power of the federal government. They believed that they could potentially be forced to compromise their principles. This group of colleges committed themselves to independence and decided not to accept these funds. They said "no" to the government.

However, now more than sixty years later, many colleges that stood against the federal government—private schools and Christian schools alike—now accept through their students some type of government funding. In fact, there remains, out of the thousands of American colleges, only a handful have resisted government funding. The rest, however, are now governed by Title IV of the current Higher Education Act. It is a document of more than 300 pages, each complete with regulations that are incomprehensible to the human mind. Senior officials of every college now governed by this act must sign a document committing themselves to compliance. Keep in mind: officials can be liable for compliance governed by a document unreadable to all but a few legal experts trained to read this document. And, as we know, the government has a tendency to expand the number of regulations when it has the power to do so. I suspect this area of law will witness the same; more bureaucratic legislation and restraints will be placed upon colleges throughout America. Never mind the fact that these codes are being written by bureaucrats who have never visited most of the campuses for which they are writing these regulations. Never mind that the officials running each school undoubtedly know better the needs and character of the school than a bureaucrat in Washington.

And the results have been disastrous. The government, in attempting to create a monopoly in higher education, has forced many to compromise or abandon altogether the principles of their founding. Quality has declined as the very purpose of education has been now changed as well. In fact, it seems that whenever the government is involved in what has historically been the responsibility of family and local community, accountability diminishes, and poor results abound. In this case, failure transcends any one level of education; colleges, high schools, and elementary schools are failing. On the occasions that the Department of Education has investigated the operations of its schools, it found immeasurable fraud of every kind. One such instance was reported in 2003 by the Office of Inspector General, revealing that the *"California Department of Education [Agreed] to Pay the United States up to $3.3 Million to Settle Whistle Blower Fraud Allegations,"* after quite the investigation that even involved FBI efforts.[39]

As of February 2023, the national student loan debt is calculated to being **$1.757 trillion.**[21] Though numerically, this figure is referred to as a report highlight, the fact of this immense volume of taxpayer's money truly amounts to being nothing but a historical lowlight—speaking volumes to the neglectful disregard associated with pitiable repayment considerations.

This is, remember, taxpayers' money. Waste, however, does not end here. As the bureaucracy overseeing education has grown, so has the duplication of jobs and inefficiency.

But there are some bright spots. As mentioned before, there are only a handful of accredited colleges in America that have decided to trust God instead of the government for their independence and perpetuity. They have foregone federal aid: Hillsdale College in Michigan. Grove City College in Pennsylvania, and New St Andrews College in Idaho are the ones I know about. I do not know much about Grove City College or New St. Andrews College, but I'm grateful for their stand.

Christian colleges should refrain from succumbing to the temptation of taking government funds. Year after year, those who do, surrender more of their freedom to the government as all kinds of regulations and legislation governing education are imposed on them. Soon they will lose their freedoms altogether. And it is, perhaps, more important that Christian colleges place their trust squarely in God's hands rather than the government's. It is the Christian schools that should know better when they place the risks that tag along with the receiving of federal money over principle. Unfortunately, many Christian colleges continue to take money from the government, and there is little prospect that they will change.

Therefore, our primary prayer has been not for you to be intelligent or wealthy but, rather, to be good. We wanted to make sure that when you left college, you would have grown in wisdom and truth and become good. After this, we would have few concerns. I do not worry about you being good spouses, fathers, neighbors, employees, employers, or citizens. It will just be part of who you are. You will be able to take positions of leadership wherever God leads you—whether in business, education, politics, or the pulpit, for your foundation will be built upon the bedrock of truth, faith, and reason. And when the rains and the winds come, you will stand firm, prepared to reclaim American society for God. I am grateful to your mother, who has been there to encourage me to work hard and serve you in the service of our Lord. What a great partner she has been. God has rewarded your mother and me tenfold by giving you to us and with the education He has directed you to. Much hard work and diligence and prayer has gone into making you the people of God you are today. I leave you this quote from Jeremiah 29:11, *"For I know the plans I have for you,' declares the Lord, 'plans to prosper you and not to harm you, plans to give you hope and a future."*

Love,
Dad

KEY TAKEAWAYS

1. Most colleges today nurture nihilism, relativism, materialism, and complacency.

2. Therefore, choose your college wisely.

X.

GUARDIANSHIP OF GOD'S RESOURCES

· · · · ·

Dear Children,

I ONCE SPOKE at a church on financial stewardship and wanted to illustrate how we can often lose because of the precepts we fail to learn and follow. We lose out by not understanding the whole counsel of God. So I asked the audience this question to see their response: "*What would you think of a person who allowed people to sell their livestock and land into servitude in exchange for food?*"

The overwhelming opinion was that such a person who would do such a thing is evil.

However, look what Genesis 47:13–21 says:

There was no food in the whole region, however, in the whole region because the famine was severe; both Egypt and Canaan wasted away because of the famine. Joseph collected all the money that was to be found in Egypt and Canaan in payment for the grain they were buying, and he brought it to Pharaoh's palace. When the money of the people of Egypt and Canaan was gone, all Egypt came to Joseph and said, "Give us food. Why should we die before your eyes? Our money is all gone." "Then bring your livestock," said Joseph. "I will sell you food in exchange for livestock, since your money is gone." So they brought their livestock to Joseph, then he gave them food in exchange for their horses, their sheep and goats, their cattle and donkeys. And he brought them through that year with food in exchange for all their livestock.

When that year was over, they came to him the following year and said, "We cannot hide from our lord the fact that since our money is gone and our livestock belongs to you, there is nothing left for our lord except our bodies and our land. Why should we perish before your eyes—we and our land as well? Buy us and our land in exchange for food, and we and our land will be in bondage to Pharaoh. Give us seed so that we may live and not die, and that the land may not become desolate." So Joseph bought all the land in Egypt for Pharaoh. The Egyptians, one and all, sold their fields, because the famine was too severe for them. The land became Pharaoh's, and Joseph reduced the people to servitude, from one end of Egypt to the other.

I am not advocating that anyone sell themselves into a life of servitude, but there is a lesson to be learned. Please take note of a few points. First, Joseph was wise. He lived in a desert in Egypt that was known to be without much water. Though God warned Joseph before the famine, it would still make sense to be prepared with food and water if you lived in a desert. The same would be true that if you lived in California, you would be prepared for an earthquake; if you lived below sea level in New Orleans, you might be concerned about flooding or hurricanes. So the first point we see is that Joseph planned ahead and was prepared for the time when the drought came. Proverbs 22:3 (NLT) tells us, "*A prudent person foresees danger and takes precautions. The simpleton goes blindly on and suffers the consequences.*"

Like many today who are not prepared, the people in Egypt and Canaan were not ready for the drought. The result was bad; these people had to sell their cattle, then their land, and eventually themselves into bondage for food. If you go back to verse 19, it says, *"Buy us and our land in exchange for food and we will be in bondage to Pharaoh. Give us **seed** so we may live and not die"* (emphasis mine).

"Give us seed," they say. Consider the year before; why did they not ask for seed? They should have asked for seed the first time so that they could plant and have a harvest at the end of the season. Like so many today, they, too, probably thought only short-term. They assumed the drought would end. But it did not.

Asking for seed at the end of the drought rather than the beginning is not wise. Joseph did not fall into this same trap as the Egyptians and Canaanites. The result? He and the king prospered. That is why these stories are there—for us to learn from others so we can avoid mistakes such as these. And we lose out when we do not read these truths. Still, sometimes, even if we do read these stories, we can easily miss the lessons that can be applied to us now.

It is important that we understand the times and circumstances and what the future may have in store. A way to do this is by understanding history. We can learn from others. If we understand history, the Word of God, human nature, and how these apply to us, then we become wise and are able to make better decisions and find safety, happiness, and prosperity. Life has peaks and valleys. Don't proceed blindly. **Joseph thought ahead, prepared, and as a result, he prospered**. We should learn from his example.

Since we do not know what the future holds, we should always be prepared for what can happen to us. Who knows what tomorrow will bring? Many continue to incur debt and become overextended, overworked, overstressed, and burned out. They assume they have secure and stable jobs.

They are not, however, prepared for times of trouble. The result, as we saw, can be disastrous.

I believe America may soon encounter another economic valley, perhaps a recession. How will consumers fare through this recession? If the choices we make today affect us tomorrow, there might be serious problems up ahead. However, there might be some who gain in such an economic downturn. It is possible that a recession will benefit those who are prepared with savings, wise investments, and few debts, just as Joseph did with grain before the famine. Then, when the economy turns bad, there will be, for these people, time to look for good opportunities. Shouldn't we be wiser than the world? Shouldn't there be more Josephs in the kingdom? Shouldn't we be the lenders rather than the debtors? Yet, daily, people sell themselves into servitude to Visa, MasterCard and high mortgage and car payments. They are forced into keeping a job they dislike. They lose by default because they have not taken the time to dig for these truths. Rather, they have acted contrary to wisdom and have taken shortcuts. Instead of this, we should walk wisely and prepare.

It is important especially that Christians act wisely and as good stewards of what they are given. In fact, Luke 16:10 makes the point that if we cannot be trusted with small things, how can we be trusted with more important things? It reads:

Whoever can be trusted with little can also be trusted with much, and whoever is dishonest with very little will also be dishonest with much. So if you have not been trustworthy in handling worldly wealth, who will trust you with true riches? And if you have not been trustworthy with someone else's property, who will give you property of your own?

The point I wish to emphasize, per the Scriptures, is that whoever can be trusted with little can also be trusted with much. If we are not trustworthy in handling worldly wealth, God will not trust us with true riches.

Likewise, if we do not handle well what God has given on Earth, He will not likely entrust us with the eternal things. It becomes clear, then, that managing worldly wealth, taking care of our families, and making wise decisions are important. And as we are trustworthy in temporal things, we will be entrusted with true riches, which have eternal benefits.

These are goals we want to work towards. In fact, as I have done business with people in leadership within the Christian church—deacons, elders, and pastors—I have noticed that many have been unwise with worldly possessions and family matters. At the same time, I have noticed that a number of these people seem to struggle within their ministries as well. Is this part of Scripture coming true? Will God trust them with more responsibility? It seems that when we are responsible with the temporal, but our focus is on the eternal, we are more alert and quicker to solve problems for both kingdoms. It is imperative, then, that we, as managers who manage those things God has entrusted us with, do it wisely so that He will entrust us with more.

Scripture speaks much more about money and finances than it is always thought to. For example, Ecclesiastes 7:12 states, "*Wisdom is a shelter as money is a shelter, but the advantage of knowledge is this: wisdom preserves those who have it.*"

This is another reason to pursue wisdom. We must embrace it and search for it like lost money or hidden treasure. It will guard us and keep us from having too much or not enough. As Solomon says in Proverbs 30:9, "[G]*ive me neither poverty nor riches, but give me only my daily bread. Otherwise, I may have too much and disown you and say, 'Who is the Lord?' Or I may become poor and steal, and so dishonor the name of my God.*"

> "I have seen something under the sun: The race is not to the swift, or the battle to the strong, nor does food come to the wise or wealth to the brilliant or favor to the learned; but time and chance happen to them all."
> **Ecclesiastes 9:11**

Ecclesiastes 2:11 gives us additional insight into finances as it compares the pursuit of worldly goods as *"a chasing after the wind."*

Then, in Ecclesiastes 5:10, we learn, *"Whoever loves money never has enough."* Whoever loves wealth, it suggests, is never satisfied. Likewise, Verse 11 states, *"As goods increase, so do those who consume them. And what benefit are they to the owners except to feast their eyes on them?"*

Then Verse 15 puts it in perspective: *"Everyone comes naked from their mother's womb, and as everyone comes, so they depart. They take nothing from their toil that they can carry in their hands."*

In verse 18, Solomon further says:

This is what I have observed to be good: that it is appropriate for a person to eat, to drink and to find satisfaction in their toilsome labor under the sun during the few days of life God has given them—for this is their lot. Moreover, when God gives someone wealth and possessions, and the ability to enjoy them, to accept their lot and be happy in their toil—this is a gift of God. They seldom reflect on the days of their life, because God keeps them occupied with gladness of heart.

This is the mindset to shoot for. This does not mean that we are to stop improving our skills or ask God to open doors. Rather, we ought to prepare for great things so God can use us more. And as gifts come and we are prepared for them, what blessings will flow! Look at Solomon; when he asked for wisdom, God gave it to him; when he made his priorities God's priorities and ruled his people well, Solomon received everything else—wealth, power, fame. It shows that when we seek wisdom, all else will often fall into place. This is why Christ tells us in Matthew chapter 6, starting with verse 25:

Therefore, I tell you, do not worry about your life, what you will eat or drink; or about your body, what you will wear. Is not life more important than food and the body more important than clothes? Look at the birds of the air; they do not sow or reap or store away in barns, and yet your Heavenly Father feeds them. Are you not much more valuable than they? Can any one of you by worrying add a single hour to your life?

*And why do you worry about clothes? See how the lilies of the field grow? They do not labor or spin. Yet I tell you that not even Solomon in all his splendor was dressed like one of these. If that is how God clothes the grass of the field which is here today and tomorrow is thrown into the fire, will He not much more clothe you, O you of little faith? So do not worry saying, "What shall we eat?" or "What shall we drink?" or "What shall we wear?" for the pagans run after all these things. And your Heavenly Father knows that you need them. **But seek first His kingdom and His righteousness, and all these things will be given to you as well.** Therefore do not worry about tomorrow, for tomorrow will worry about itself. Each day has enough trouble of its own* (emphasis mine).

Do the right thing in your own life, and God will provide what you need. In no way is this a defense of the "health and wealth" doctrine or the "name it and claim it" Christianity that one often sees on TV. God is not our own personal concierge who simply takes our orders and fulfills them immediately. Rather, He is a father to Whom we pray and ask for His will in our lives. God will often not give an audible sign or response to our prayers, for He works in mysterious ways and in ways that are not always clear to those who pray. Still, it is important that we do not approach prayer as a way to bend God's will. Ask that God's will be done in all circumstances, then work hard, make right decisions, and do all that you can to pursue the right things.

In my own case, your mother and I always prayed with a tone of *"Please, if it is Your will."* When we wanted a house, we first prayed and then did everything we could through using scriptural principles like tithing, hard work, being skilled in what we do, and paying close attention to the things that work. It took us years and much effort before we bought the house we wanted. But in the end, we waited upon God, and He provided in His time. While we must boldly believe God's promises and follow them, we must also keep in mind all that He has to say and have the discipline to implement it in our lives. This is the recipe for true success, although we are not guaranteed financial success. As we will discuss later in this book, there are things more important than money when it comes to success. That includes a purpose and calling upon our lives, and you may be called upon someday to give it all to a worthy cause: to our God, our country, or our family.

There is also great comfort in that throughout history, there are examples of God giving to His people before they even ask for it. We should remember that He is attentive to our needs and is looking out for our interests. He likes to give good gifts to those who follow Him. But we must decide whether or not we will be faithful. It is our choice. Deuteronomy 8:11–14 and 17–19 (Revised Standard Version) explain this perspective:

Take heed lest you forget the Lord, your God, by not keeping His commandments and His ordinances and His statutes . . . lest when you have eaten and are full and have built large houses and live in them and when your herds and flocks multiply and your silver and gold is multiplied and all that you have is multiplied, then your heart will be lifted up and you forget the Lord, your God . . .

Beware, lest you say in your heart, "My power and the might of my hand have gotten me this wealth." You shall remember the Lord, your God, for it is He who gives you the power to get wealth, that He may confirm His covenant which He swore to your fathers as at this day. And if you forget the Lord, your God, and go after other gods and serve them and worship them, I solemnly warn you this day that you shall surely perish.

Though this promise was made under the covenant between the Israelites and God, we should learn from the principle contained within it. God is just, and because of this, He will punish those who do wrong and reward those who do right. This is especially true as you review the advice to Israel in the book of Deuteronomy, containing thirty-four chapters and over fifty warnings.

In fact, in my own life, I have seen God work in incredible ways. To show this, I would like to share with you some of my personal experiences that have helped me through life.

My father was a policeman. We moved around a few times as I was growing up and lived in and out of different homes and apartments. My dad and mom were high school dropouts. Consequently, my dad was happy if I could simply graduate from high school with at least a C average. The bar was not set very high. I did make it through high school with about a C-minus average, knowing that this was all that was required. I had not prepared for success. In my late teens and early twenties, my friends would joke, saying, "It took Morrell seven years to get through high school." Some were critical of me. That is okay. I deserved it. However, when I got married, I suddenly had to consider the needs of another person, and I began to feel squeezed. I sobered up quickly and realized the importance of marriage and that having kids would multiply my expenses. At the same time, your mother's priority and desire was to stay at home and invest in her children.

> *"Better a little with the fear of the Lord than great wealth with turmoil."*
> **Proverbs 15:16**

Those were turning points in my life. And as I muddled through these years as a young businessman, I began concentrating on the book of Proverbs, which was a huge part of my getting through the years that were soon to follow. By 1982, still young and newly married, interest rates began to climb, and home mortgages hit 19 percent. As you might imagine, sales came to a halt. Convincing a consumer to purchase a home at 19 percent mortgage was not an easy task. I saw real estate and mortgage offices close. Needless to say, the industry shrank. Concerned for the future, I drafted a resumé so I could go job hunting. After that, I bought a Snapper lawn mower. My thought was that on weekends, I could pick up extra cash mowing lawns. How funny it is now when you consider my lack of mechanical expertise. I can barely rake a lawn let alone mow one. But it was the way that I was going to deal with this 19 percent market: I would get out of the business and find a new career.

One day in the midst of these economic conditions, there came more discouraging news. As I listened to the radio, I heard that the California real estate industry had reached its lowest point since the Great Depression of 1929. I was overwhelmed as I thought about the business I was in. I called Joanie and said, "Be praying about me switching careers soon." She informed me that morning, however, after a visit to the doctor, that she was pregnant. She said, "You'll need to stay in your job another seven or eight months because we need the health insurance benefits." We had little money saved at this point in our lives.

But the worst was yet to come. The company I was employed with, a good and decent company, had been doing business with a company of bad reputation, and it appeared as though our company was owned by this other company. That company had been doing business fraudulently. Eventually, the Justice Department investigated that company and brought charges against them. They then investigated the company I was employed with. One day, they came to our office requesting everybody to leave the premises. Trash cans were tipped over and files emptied onto the middle of the floor (fortunately, our company was exonerated of all charges). But, in the meantime, as a salesman for this company, I had to deal with all the negative press. In fact, my competition went so far as to pass out newspaper clippings of the troubles we were in to my clients. They were attempting to run me out of business.

So here I was stuck in the worst real estate market since the Great Depression, my wife was pregnant, with no money, and my competition using bad press about my company against me. It was a string of bad luck that rarely happens. It was, you might say, a perfect storm. So I registered my complaint with God and asked Him, why all the grief? That small, still voice spoke to my mind and said, *"Now, you've been reading the Scriptures, particularly Proverbs, things about keeping a good name, being skilled in your craft, seeking counsel, and working diligently."*

I then recalled the Scripture I had read before, which said, *He who works with a diligent hand will prosper* (a paraphrase of Proverbs 10:4). As I thought this through, I realized that it does not say, *He who works with a diligent hand will prosper providing interest rates stay under 12, 10, 9, or 8 percent, or providing that you are not in a recession or an inflationary period, or that your company is tanking and getting bad press.* Rather, it simply says that if you work diligently, then you will prosper. I took this verse to heart and kept it always in my mind. Other verses came to mind as well, such as Proverbs 16:3: *"Commit to the Lord whatever you do, and He will establish your plans."*

I had determined that day I would do just that, for I had no alternative. I put in a few extra hours, more effort, and prayed harder. Approximately ten months later, somehow, amazingly, I set a company sales record despite the high interest rates and all the other external difficulties of the business. I think part of my success came when my competitors, discouraged by the situation, gave up. The pie, you might say, had shrunk. There was no longer much business out there. Instead of working harder, my competition ended up at the local bars around three in the afternoon, crying the blues with each other. Realizing this, I knew I had to take the pieces of the pie they were not working for. As they cried the blues and drank, I worked. It was a tremendous lesson (however, it is one that I would not like to experience again).

Since then, many of my fears have been alleviated. This lesson reminded me that God is in control and that His Word should help us to be strong enough to withstand the difficult circumstances. The result was that I prospered during a difficult period of life. I prayed, worked hard, and moved forward. I found that God is bigger than the economy or our circumstances. I needed to be faithful and trust Him. If He is for us, who can be against us? No one and nothing. Not even a bad economy. Since then, I have had more confidence in His advice. As Proverbs 30:5 says, *"Every word of God is flawless."*

No, things don't always work out. Sometimes we have to learn that God is teaching us lessons, but we can trust Him through difficult circumstances and improve our character. Our odds increase as we try to follow the advice in Scriptures.

Just like God gave Joseph advice, He gives us advice. So work hard, and you will do well. Life is a risk, and we need to conquer it rather than it conquering us. Those times made me a better man. Amen.

I would also like to share with you some of the verses that helped me back then so that you may see how useful these words are. Proverbs 22:29 says, *"You see a man skilled in his craft, he will stand before kings."*

And how do kings pay? Very well. Proverbs 12:24, 13:4, and 21:5 tell us to work hard, for it is the diligent who will attain wealth. The diligent will rule, and the diligent are satisfied. And the plans of the diligent lead to profit. As Proverbs 14:23 says, *"All hard work brings a profit."*

Notice it says, *"All hard work."* Not "some hard work." Likewise, *"All hard work brings a profit but mere talk leads only to poverty."*

This is Scripture, and we ought not to forget what it says about these things.

Take this example: I know a gentleman who is CEO of a bank with forty branches. Though he has talent and intelligence, it has not been these that have propelled him to run one of the most successful business banks in America. What got him there has been discipline and hard work. He is an ex-Marine, but as he showed time and time again - the discipline of a true Marine never expires. While there are many smart men and women in the banking field—smarter than he and with more talents—none that I know have more discipline or a better work ethic. He has the ability to persevere and stay focused on the job at hand. I am very impressed with him because I know he has attained these things more through those characteristics than anything else. And this should be a matter of hope to us—with hard work we can all achieve more than we would likely imagine. The only other option is laziness and poverty.

As Proverbs 10:4 says, *"Lazy hands make a man poor but the diligent hands bring wealth."* You must either work hard or be lazy. Just make sure you remember which leads to which.

In addition to hard work, it is always important to keep a good reputation. As Proverbs says, *"A good name is to be desired more than riches."*

In fact, ever since I was a young man in the business world, I have worked hard to maintain a good reputation. When I first entered the business, I was told just the opposite, that one had to be deceptive to get ahead. Although I was naïve and had a propensity to walk on the dark side, I believed this Scripture and made an effort to follow it. In the end, it has proven to be profitable. People trust me and bring their business to me because of this trust. Do not underestimate the power of a good name.

Another important Proverb tells us, *"Plans fail for lack of counsel, but with many advisers they succeed"* (Prov. 15:22). Over the years, as I have faced difficult decisions, I have sought out people smarter than myself and have learned to ask good questions. I had a business coach who helped me work through difficult decisions. I also have mentors for other areas of my life and have been saved much grief by having them. I found that it is a very good thing to have wise people around you, whether to give you counsel concerning your relationship with your spouse or to teach you how to raise your children. It is difficult to overestimate the importance of finding a mentor.

In fact, I had a friend named Tom who had raised four fine young men. When it came to family matters, I would call Tom from time to time, asking him questions about how I could do a better job as a father and husband. In business, I joined a mentoring group of business owners. I noticed that while there were many talented people in our group, there were also some with very little talent. One of the latter category, nearly in bankruptcy, joined our group. He humbled himself and sought counsel. He listened to other members of the group and asked questions. Today, this young man is becoming exceedingly wealthy—and it is not by his talent. Rather, he is succeeding because he humbled himself, took time to listen, sought advice from those wiser than himself, and then applied it. I can think of many other examples of people just like him. These have taught me to stay humble and seek counsel. In a multitude of counselors, there is indeed victory.

> "Life is a grindstone, whether it grinds you down or polishes you up depends on what you are made of."
> **Author Unknown**

Next, I'd like to share a verse that gives me clarity and hope for the future. Ecclesiastes 9:11 says, *"The race is not to the swift or the battle to the strong, nor does food come to the wisest or wealth to the brilliant or favor to the learned; but time and chance happen to them all."*

It has been interesting to see the truth of this verse played out in life. I have seen not-so-smart people make much money. Sometimes things that look like disadvantages are not disadvantages at all but opportunities for success. I have seen that intelligence and talent are not always a requirement for success. Rather, it is how we use what God has given us. This is why there is always hope, even for the less swift. In fact, I would count myself among these—and that is not false humility. Anyone who knows me will confirm this. But there has been a transformation. Any success I can claim can be directly linked back to reading and following His Word.

Here is a list of a few key verses that you should keep at the forefront of your mind:

- Proverbs 22:7 tells us debt is a curse: *"The rich rule over the poor, and the borrower is slave to the lender."*
- Deuteronomy chapter 8 also claims debt is a curse. If you cannot afford it, do not buy it. It may not be God's will or the right timing. Put your pride aside and use discipline and restraint and say, "No." Wait patiently. Do not ever praise God for material items if you are paying interest to credit card companies for them. When God gives to His children, they do not come with high interest rates.
- Ecclesiastes 9:10: *"Whatever you do, do it with all your might."*
- 1 Timothy 6:6: *"But Godliness with contentment is great gain."*

Remember that it is not money that makes the man or woman. Follow the example of Paul, who learned to be content in both good times and bad. Do not let materialism be the desire of your heart. Be content in whatever circumstances God places you. As Proverbs 23:4 says, *"Do not weary yourself to get rich."*

Keep things in proper perspective. Live in moderation. If you are always tiring yourself, and it is becoming a pattern, you are becoming a workaholic. Stop it.

- Proverbs 11:28: *"Those who trust in their riches will fall, but the righteous will thrive like a green leaf."*
- Proverbs 13:4: *"A sluggard's appetite is never filled, but the desires of the diligent are fully satisfied."*
- Proverbs 13:11: *"Dishonest money dwindles away, but whoever gathers money little by little makes it grow."*
- Psalms 37:25–26: *"I have been young and now I am old, yet I have not seen the righteous forsaken or his descendants begging bread. All*

day long He is gracious and lends, and His descendants are a blessing" (NASB).

We find in Scripture that those who are not righteous, those who are dishonest, do not prosper. Look at the Scriptures related to this theme:

> *"Sow your seeds in the morning and at evening, let not your hands be idle for you do not know which will succeed whether this or that or whether both will do equally well."*
> **Ecclesiastes 11:9**

+ Proverbs 13:21: *"Trouble pursues the sinner, but the righteous are rewarded with good things."*
+ Proverbs 15:27: *"The greedy bring ruin to their households, but the one who hates bribes will live."*
+ Proverbs 20:4: *"Sluggards do not plow in season; so at harvest time they look but find nothing."*
+ Proverbs 28:19: *"Those who work their land will have abundant food, but those who chase fantasies will have their fill of poverty."*
+ Proverbs 28:25: *"The greedy stir up conflict, but those who trust in the Lord will prosper."*
+ Proverbs 27:23–24: *"Be sure you know the condition of your flocks; give careful attention to your herds for riches do not endure forever."*
+ Proverbs 23:4: *"Do not wear yourself out to get rich; do not trust in your own cleverness. Cast but a glance at riches, and they are gone, for they will surely sprout wings and fly off to the sky like an eagle."*

Conversely, look at the promises of Scripture:

+ Proverbs 16:3: *"Commit to the Lord whatever you do, and He will establish your plans."*

- Proverbs 16:20: *"Whoever gives heed to instruction prospers, and blessed is the one who trusts in the Lord."*
- Proverbs 19:8: *"The one who gets wisdom loves life; the one who cherishes understanding will soon prosper."*
- Proverbs 21:5: *"The plans of the diligent lead to profit as surely as haste leads to poverty."*
- Proverbs 21:21: *"Whoever pursues righteousness and love finds life, prosperity and honor."*

These are great things to remember as you live your life and pursue what God has for you. The goal is to aim for a life well spent.

Love,
Dad

Key Takeaways

1. *Think ahead. Be prepared.*

2. *Trust God.*

3. *Diligence pays off.*

4. *Be humble.*

5. *Keep a good reputation.*

6. *Moderation.*

XI

FINANCE 101

· · · · · ·

"Let the temporal things serve your use but the eternal be the object of your desire."
—Thomas a' Kempis

Dear Children,

HAVING BEEN IN the finance and real estate business for decades, I have had the opportunity to observe what has worked and what has not worked financially in the lives of many people. I have studied and interacted with these people and have come to see an array of spending habits, money management tendencies, and financial mistakes and successes. Additionally, I have devoted much time to studying how to make money according to both the worldly and biblical perspective. Therefore, I hope my insights are profitable.

When considering the topic of finances, we must ask an important question: Does one have to make a lot of money in order to feel like a human being or to feel good about oneself? The answer is "No." It is fine to make good money, but it is certainly not a requirement to live well.

However, the way the world carries on about money, you would think that money is all there is. Magazines, newspapers, and television shows have taught us to view people like Warren Buffett, Bill Gates, Jeff Bezos, Mark Zuckerberg, and other rich and famous celebrities as today's heroes.

In reality, people are more than physical beings, and riches only satisfy needs derived from believing the very opposite of this fact. Of course, people need money to exist. However, we also have a soul that nothing in the material world can completely satisfy. It is important that we never lose sight of this. Remember that if you work eight hours a day, you will spend approximately one-third of your life providing for yourself and your family. This is why we must find the proper balance between work and the rest of life, finances, and spiritual things.

The Bible teaches us that finances are worthy of our attention: there are over **2,000 Scriptures** on the subject of money. Likewise, we see tens of thousands of books in popular culture devoted to this subject, each representing one of the endless opinions out there. We must learn how to think about finances if we are to live well.

Having worked in the world of business for many years, I have seen that the way people manage their finances either sets them free or enslaves them. Finance is a difficult subject to learn well. But I have come to learn that if one is disciplined, able to keep his ego in check, wise with what God has entrusted, and able to recognize that material blessings are temporal and that the goal in life is to become good rather than rich, this person will be served well and will have lived out the basic principles of finance.

So let us begin with the tale of two cities: *the city of God and the city of man*. By the city of God, I mean the eternal Heaven; by the city of man, I mean the temporal world. Why the two? There exists a tension between the two: we live in one while hoping for the other. We want to serve God, but we also desire to live well in the city of man. St. Augustine once spoke about this dynamic and described the struggle humanity faces in attempting to balance both. He said that cities on Earth often lack justice because people are driven by greed or the desire for more than what is necessary. In short, people are not prone to living in financial moderation. Rather, greed, avarice, and materialism tend to destroy the earthly city and, in doing so, the individual as well.

How this happens is simple: the flesh, in its desire for material possessions, ceaselessly produces desires, which eventually lead to excess, and excess leads to injustice. Consequently, Augustine refers to Galatians 5:17 (KJV): *"The flesh lusteth against the spirit."* How true. These things wage war within us. They create a tension that cannot be eradicated on Earth but can be kept in balance. And this should be our goal: to thread the needle between fulfilling needs and pursuing excesses. And Augustine offers a way to do this: the virtue of moderation, which itself requires morality and restraint.

These are the keys for living in peace, prosperity, and justice: the ability to moderate one's earthly desires and restraint in pursuing material goods. Additionally, as human beings recognize their place before God, they then tend to deny themselves and reach a lifestyle of moderation. Then citizens bring glory to the earthly city as well as the Heavenly.

This does not mean, however, that because one is not excessive, he is moderate. As Augustine warns in *The City of God against the Pagans*, *"Behold, however, the man who lives as he desires because he has forced and commanded himself not to desire what he cannot have, but to choose only what he can have."*[5]

True moderation is when a person can have things but chooses to pursue only those which he needs.

Aristotle as well saw that an overzealous pursuit of material goods would create in a person an insatiable appetite for more goods. This, in turn, would cause a person to end up in a downward spiral. The antidote to this is virtue, a quality of the soul. Like Augustine, Aristotle believed it was moderation, combined with the rest of the virtues, that would lead to humanity's ultimate happiness. Conversely, the opposite of virtue—vice—will lead to ultimate suffering and unhappiness. In this case, the immoderate pursuit of money will result in a state for which people were not created. As 1 Timothy 6:10 states, *"For the love of money is a root of all kinds of evil. Some people, eager for money, have wandered from the faith and pierced themselves with many griefs."*

It is important to point out that this verse is often used to suggest that money or the pursuit of it is inherently wrong. However, this verse says no such thing. Money is not bad; it is an inanimate object without a will. It is people who have a will, and that means we are the ones who are capable of being bad. So what is important when dealing with money is how *we* control it, how *we* allow it to control us, or the extent to which *we* pursue it. The problem lies in us, not money. It is *our* eagerness for money that has caused some, according to this passage, to wander from the faith and pierce themselves with many griefs. If we can control ourselves, then money is no longer a cause for sin.

So how *do* we live in moderation, which, according to Aristotle, is necessary to *"the good life?"* One short answer is that we must remember that we are here on Earth briefly and that, while it is a fine thing to make money, it must not keep us from our focus on the eternal. But because this is the fundamental question on this subject, I will devote the rest of the chapter to the long answer.

> "A wise man should have money in his head but not in his heart."
> **Jonathan Swift**

So why do some people succeed while others fail? I have worked over the years with literally tens of thousands of clients. Many we have been able to help, while others we could not. We have seen those who have managed well and those who have not. Of all of the clients we have worked with who have had serious financial difficulties, I have noticed that the overwhelming majority have violated scriptural principles governing money management. Of course, sometimes there are problems brought on by forces outside of their control. However, out of the thousands I have worked with, I can only recall two or three clients for whom this was true. The rest, unfortunately, were in situations that were a direct result of their own mistakes (though many placed themselves into the ranks of those whose situations were outside of their control). **Frequently, these people, lacking knowledge from both scriptural and human nature perspectives, had made wrong decisions that placed them in harm's way.** Often, they lacked discipline, or their pride interfered with the better choice. Unfortunately, I saw this pattern both within and outside of the Christian community.

In the early 1990s, my good friend Dennis came to work alongside me. While he was here, another employee, Tom, became friends with Dennis and helped to convince him that it was essential to have a relationship with God. After much time and thought, Dennis committed his life to God. Among the many changes Dennis underwent in this was a new way that he viewed his finances.

One day, Dennis approached me and said he wanted to advertise on a local Christian radio station. I responded that I would prefer not to do that. I always had a twinge of guilt trying to get business from the faith community. But Dennis, being a new believer, said he preferred to work with fellow believers and to begin to help them manage their finances better. Though I was skeptical, he said these magic words, "I will pay for half of the ad." I took advantage of this opportunity—one that would open my eyes to a startling fact.

What I found was that many of our fellow believers were saddled with debt as much as the non-religious community. Many that I saw were living paycheck to paycheck and had little, if any, financial restraint or management. In fact, the Barna Research Group—which accumulates polling data, studies the habits of Christians and compares their lifestyles with those of the secular world—came to a similar conclusion. [24] Their research has shown that there is little distinction between Christians and non-Christians in everything from the way they divorce to the way they tithe. I have certainly found this to be true in the way Christians manage money. We, too, buy too much, pay too much, have too much credit card debt, and have become too encumbered by the things of this world, all while Hebrews 12:1 admonishes us to run the race of life unencumbered. All too often, we have allowed the culture to impact us more than we have impacted culture. We conform very nicely to the patterns of this world despite the commands of Scripture to do otherwise: Romans 12:2 commands us, *"Do not conform to the pattern of this world, but be transformed by the renewing of our mind."*

Scripture also tells us debt is a curse. It's hard to run the race of life unencumbered as we're instructed to do when we're carrying a load of bricks in a backpack. And if each brick represents some type of monetary note that you have—Visa, Master Card, or otherwise—it's difficult. Have the restraint and discipline to say no to these things.

Will Rogers once said, *"Too many people spend money they haven't earned to buy things they don't want to impress people they don't like."* How true is that? Often, us, men, are driven by our egos. We buy things with money we don't have just to impress people. One of my biggest downfalls has been trying to impress people that I have "arrived." And I have learned that at the end of the day, when you do try to impress people, they think either you're arrogant or, if they believe that you're well off, they're often envious. Neither one of those are good. If anything, keep silent about your finances and keep people guessing. And usually they'll guess that you are doing better than you really are. It's good to not always show your cards. It's the humpback whale who gets harpooned. And when people think you have things, they'll take potshots at you. So you have to keep that in check.

Avoid all those things that can get you in trouble. Trust God. Allow Him to open the doors as He sees fit and close the doors that would be harmful to you and your family. Let your prayer be, *"God, let me only have this thing if I can pay cash for it and if it doesn't cause me or others to stumble or hinders my walk with You or my time away from my wife and children."*

Put your pride aside. Pride goes before destruction, and a haughty spirit before a fall.

As a side note, I do think that we need a certain amount of ambition to open a business, run for office, or lead troops into battle. But there's a point when that ambition can cross over into pride. So tread carefully.

If we are not renewing our mind according to the Word of God, then we will be transformed by the world. We become conformed to the patterns of this world in all areas, including finances. We spend what we do not have with a "go now and pay later" mentality. We do not wait on the Lord for his provision, but rather we beseech Visa and Master Card to deliver the fulfillment of our desires. In short, the world is impacting us, and we do nothing to stop it. We buy bigger homes, bigger cars, bigger boats. And the list goes on. The only antidote to this is found in developing a clear perspective on God's Word. Only then can we avoid having our mind conformed to the patterns of the world, which, by the way, only lead to endless pursuits and elusive fulfillments.

Take this, for example: Americans today live better than people of any country in any age have ever lived before. Today you live better than any counterpart you might have in the entire world. Are we satisfied? Has happiness increased? I would say no. Instead, each fulfillment of a material want has only given birth to new desires. We do not focus on what we have but what we want. And it is this endless pursuit that causes discontentment and financial difficulties despite the general affluence of our age. As previously mentioned, a top reason for divorce involves disagreements and problem relating to money. Why, especially amid such prosperity? Do we not have enough to live? Of course, we have enough. But it is immoderation and the pursuit of material fulfillment that has pushed us toward financial and familial ruin.

We must remember that the world is cunning and that we have become willing partners in the growth of materialism. It is no secret that the marketing industry focuses on careful research in exhausting the finds for ways to sell their products, no matter how subtle. In fact, a 2015 article from Red Crow Marketing reports that average Americans are exposed to commercials in the thousands per day—between 4,000 and 10,000, according to digital experts.[28] This finding was nearly a decade ago and is possibly a severe understatement compared to present-day advertisement exposures through endless marketing avenues, including television, newspapers, magazines, radio, internet surfing, and mobile app use. Even a simple drive down the street is likely to encounter a billboard or vehicles sporting advertisement decals for business and local deals.

This is why we must be vigilant. We must be aware of what is bombarding us, even if we cannot stop the bombardment, for the point of advertising is to encourage us to reach into our pockets and purchase more things. To assist us in this, even when we do not have the money to spend, credit card companies encourage us to buy by promising us nice things like air miles and cash back. While we rack up these air miles, however, we are charged rates of over **16.9 percent.** Even consumers like myself, who think that we have outsmarted the credit card companies by paying off our credit cards monthly, are likely to spend an average of 27 percent more using credit cards. It is the lenders who are rewarded at our expense. The billions of dollars spent annually by these companies on advertisements laced with catchy slogans and the promise of rewards are quickly made up and surpassed by our response to them, which is to spend.

The results of overspending can be disastrous. Back in the early 2000s, overspending was at crisis levels, but few could see it for what it was. In 2007, I wrote down my thoughts on the state of the economy, and looking back, I think my observations were correct:

This problem, which is a serious one, also shows itself in another area: real estate. For example, in 2003, homeowners refinanced their homes at the fastest pace ever. Remember the Ditech, Green Tree, and the Money Store commercials? Well, consumers took money out of their homes and used it to pay off more consumer debt than ever before. This is why 2005 became the second most profitable year in history for the mortgage industry: countless homeowners used mortgage companies to refinance their homes and take money out to pay off credit card debt. But here is where the facts get interesting. According to the Consumer's Banking Association, over 70 percent of those who refinanced in 2005 also refinanced in 2003. However, at the end of 2005, consumers still had more credit card debt than ever before. The story does not end there.

In 2005, Americans had a .05 percent negative rate of savings, which was less than what people saved during the Great Depression. Then, in 2006, we saved even less than 2005 at a negative 1 percent rate, the worst amount of saving since 1934. What does this mean? It means that although Americans refinanced to pay off debt at some of the highest rates in history, they ended up at the end of the year with more debt and less savings and broke records doing it. At the same time, foreclosures are increasing at an alarming rate. All of this cannot be good for America.

Today, as I write, America has just come through a real estate boom, particularly in California, where there is a small supply and high demand. We were told that prices would never go down. However, things are beginning to change. Builders are nervous as many are beginning to sit on three years' worth of inventory. Since they cannot sell their homes anymore at the price they need, they are giving generous incentives, everything from paying the borrower's closing costs to landscaping upgrades to swimming pools. Likewise, subprime lenders are in trouble after years of making risky loans. Since the beginning of 2007, approximately ninety national lenders have either gone out of business or have filed for bankruptcy protection. No one knows what will happen, even in real estate. But we do know that it is easy to upset the balance. Unemployment could go up. The price of oil could go up. We could have a major war. No one knows when calamity will strike. Although we are often given little warning for these things, God gives us His Word and, through it, gives us good advice to withstand storms that

*will come our way. Therefore, we must prepare and be good stewards in
the short term so that things in the long term will take care of themselves.*

Of course, within a year or so of that writing, the housing bubble burst,
and the world ended up in the worst recession since the Great Depression.

I'm a short-term pessimist but a long-term optimist about the future
and the economy. The reason is that the rules and principles of life remain
the same. These do not change. Therefore, if we build our foundations
on solid economic principles, review the numbers, do the math, and read
God's Word to solidify our base, we will succeed. Earlier, I discussed the
passage in Romans 12:2 about not being conformed to this world but being
transformed. The second half of that verse confirms that as we are transformed, we will gain the ability to discern His perfect will for our lives. As
it says, *"Then you will be able to test and approve what God's will is—His good,
pleasing and perfect will."* If you want to know God's will, whether it be in
marriage, raising children, or managing finances, then read God's Word.

Over the years, the two most common mistakes relate to how we spend
and how we invest. Consequently, it seems that we must learn how to spend
wisely, buy wisely, save wisely, and place our money into wise investments.
But how do we do this? There are many opinions on the subject. Countless
books and magazine articles have been written on the subject. Both CNN
and Fox News have shows on money and finance. Much of these are good
sources whose materials should be read. In my own life, I have spent time
improving my sales techniques by studying Zig Ziglar, Tommy Hawkins,
and Brian Tracy. Even these experts have varying opinions. So who is right?
Whose advice should we follow? The answer is God's. Here is why.

Those Madison Avenue marketers are smart. Many of them have MBAs
from prestigious colleges and universities, and their job is to use "marketing
hooks" to encourage us to part with our money and purchase their products.
They work on this throughout the day. It is easy to get sucked in. So how do
we counter this barrage of information and become wise and use restraint?

The answer is that we must develop good habits in our lives. The first and foremost foundational principle is paying close attention to the Word of God and all it has to say in it. God knows our hearts and understands that we are easily deceived into wrong thinking and actions. Consider Proverbs 1:7, which tells us that the first matter of importance is not money but rather obtaining wisdom, *"The fear of the Lord is the beginning of wisdom."*

We are under the watchful eye of God, so we must deal truthfully and uprightly. This does not mean that we will not sin, but it does mean that we must give our best effort to living rightly. And this is the path to wisdom. Proverbs 1:2 tells us that wisdom gives one the ability to understand *"words of insight."* This is right decision-making. Common sense today is becoming very uncommon, especially in financial decision-making. It is wisdom that we need in order to do this well. Proverbs 2:9 says that wisdom will help us to understand *"what is right and just and fair."* This generally results in good financial gain as well as stability in relationships. Proverbs 2 also says wisdom guards one's heart and mind, as well as our relationships and financial decisions. Proverbs, if followed, gives us probabilities of success. Proverbs 3:2 further encourages its readers that wisdom *"will prolong your life many years and bring you peace and prosperity."* Proverbs 3:14–15 says more about this, teaching us that wisdom *"is more profitable than silver and yields better returns than gold. She is more precious than rubies; nothing you desire can compare with her."*

Once again, God understands our nature and uses terminology that attracts our attention in order to show us the value of wisdom; it is, He says, more **profitable** than silver, and it has greater **returns** than gold. Wisdom **yields** things to us. It **profits** us and **returns** to us better percentages than that of **silver,** and **rubies.** God is not trying to sound like a financial planner, but He is showing us that returns in life are better as we draw closer to Him and begin to understand His wisdom rather than ours.

God desires us to prosper more than just financially; He wants us to prosper mentally and spiritually as well. These texts help us understand

His heart's desire for our lives. Notice Proverbs 4, verses 7–18, which lends additional clarity as to the benefit of wisdom,

Get wisdom, get understanding; do not forsake my words or turn away from them. Do not forsake wisdom, and she will protect you; love her, and she will watch over you. The beginning of wisdom is this: Get wisdom. Though it cost all you have, get understanding. Cherish her, and she will exalt you; embrace her, and she will honor you. She will give you a garland to grace your head and present with you with a glorious crown.

Listen, my son, accept what I say, and the years of your life will be many. I instruct you in the way of wisdom and lead you along straight paths. When you walk, your steps will not be hampered; when you run, you will not stumble. Hold on to instruction, do not let it go; guard it well, for it is your life. Do not set foot on the path of the wicked or walk in the way of evildoers. Avoid it, do not travel on it; turn from it and go on your way. For they cannot rest until they do evil; they are robbed of sleep till they make someone stumble. They eat the bread of wickedness and drink the wine of violence. The path of the righteous is like the morning sun, shining ever brighter till the full light of day.

Verses 20–27 continue,

My son, pay attention to what I say; turn your ear to my words. Do not let them out of your sight, keep them within your heart; for they are life to those who find them and health to one's whole body. Above all else, guard your heart, for everything you do flows from it. Keep your mouth free from perversity; keep corrupt talk far from your lips. Let your eyes look straight ahead; fix your gaze directly before you. Give careful thought to the paths for your feet and be steadfast in all your ways. Do not turn to the right or to the left; keep your foot from evil.

It is straightforward: **Wisdom is more important than wealth.** Have wisdom, and your desire for wealth will be put in its proper place among the rest of your desires. Of course, it is not a bad thing to work hard and attain wealth, but this should never be the ultimate goal in life. In fact, it is when one actually obtains wealth and the power that comes with it that one question becomes ever more important: how am I to use this? And the inability to answer this question is, sadly, most evident in the lives of young movie stars and musicians who have money and fame, yet make their lives into public train wrecks. They go through rehab fighting drug and alcohol addiction, among many other things. These people have pierced themselves because they have lacked wisdom and were not prepared to answer the profound questions that inevitably come with wealth and power. They have pursued wealth but not the improvement of their souls.

Likewise, I have also seen friends and associates who have walked away from the faith because money inflated their pride, and the world lured them into a spiritual slumber. These, too, have pierced themselves. Not everyone is prepared to handle wealth, let alone true riches. That is why God reminds us to be content with what we have. Does not life consist of more than just temporal possessions? Contentment is a good antidote to avarice. Proverbs continues, *"My son, do not forget my teaching, but keep my commands in your heart, for they will prolong your life many years and bring you peace and prosperity"* (Prov. 3:1–2).

This is what wisdom does. It helps us stand against those Madison Avenue marketers and all the other temptations that come our way. It is a great thing that there is hope even for a fool—a fool such as me. Consider starting in Psalm 119:130: *"The unfolding of your words gives light; it gives understanding to the simple."* Or Proverbs 8:5: *"You who are simple, gain prudence."* Psalm 116:6: *"The Lord preserves the simple"* (NASB). And Psalm 19:7: *"The statutes of the Lord are trustworthy, making wise the simple."*

How much more will God be able to help the wise? If I have any amount of temporal success, I can link it back to the Word of God. These ancient texts have given me insight. The book of Proverbs has over one hundred Scriptures regarding wealth building that have helped me in business. It is a great place to start regarding money management.

However, I must depart from the so-called "health and wealth doctrine," whose proponents claim that you are guaranteed financial success and good health if you follow God. I would say that hard work and following the advice laid out for us is necessary to this type of success, but it is not always sufficient. Sometimes we will be blessed in other ways that are not financial. Still, we have a treasure in Scripture that we should follow. It is the best way to live and the only means to true happiness. God understands our hearts and weaknesses, as well as our own deceptive thinking and how the world seduces us. He knows what we are faced with on a daily basis. I believe God would prefer to see His children prosper but in ways not always involving money. There are things much more important than money. The key is to make God's priorities our priorities. We should, as Jesus says in Matthew 6:33, "*Seek first His kingdom and His righteousness,*" and all else will fall into place. You will find that this will shift our focus away from money to God, from the material things to the high and noble things. It places us on the path to God and His will for our lives.

As I reflect on the best times of my life, it has always been more about family, relationships, inspirational times with God, and being around likeminded people. Those times have brought me more joy and purpose than any of the material things ever could. Wisdom gets a person to a point where they realize they do not need things. So the number-one building block is to pursue as much as possible the heart and mind of God, which requires paying close attention to His Word.

Love,

Dad

Key Takeaways

1. *Find balance between work and intangibles.*

2. *Focus on eternal principles given in Scripture.*

3. *Be disciplined. Subordinate ego.*

4. *Material wealth is temporal.*

5. *Attain moderation.*

The habit of saving money requires more force of character than most people have developed, for the reason that saving means self-denial and sacrifice of amusements and pleasures in scores of different ways."
**Napoleon Hill,
The Laws of Success (1928)**

XII.

INVESTING VERSUS SPECULATING

· · · · ·

Dear Children,

HERE ARE A few bullet points about the subject of investing.

Though the market has been a tremendous force for wealth creation in our time, this comes with a caveat: the market has produced more speculators than investors. And this is a dangerous scenario—namely because of what speculators typically do.

A speculator is one who buys a property with poor financing in order to keep the payments low. Consider, for example, that a loan amount of $500,000 at a 9.5 percent interest rate would make your full payment $4,190. So if this is your rate, and you are a speculator trying to rent this property out at, let's say, $2,500 a month, you will have a $1,690 per month negative cash flow, which does not include the cost of repairs and other unforeseen problems. Under this scenario, you are not investing; you are speculating. You are carrying too big of a negative with only the hope that your property will increase in value at a rate faster than 9.5 percent a year. Since this is unlikely, it is a dangerous business to be in. This is why it is better to invest. Let me describe for you even more what this looks like.

The premier stock investor and second wealthiest man in the world, Warren Buffett, with a net worth of over $100 billion, has spread his wealth over many solid companies. Mr. Buffett had a mentor named Benjamin Graham, who wrote the book titled *The Intelligent Investor.*[20] Speculating, according to Graham, is essentially sophisticated gambling or, at best, intelligent guessing. You get a hot tip and bet on it just like you would a race. You are not sure what the outcome will be. Many pick stocks and invest in real estate the same way. Everybody wants to get in on a hot stock or a booming real estate market. The bottom line is that some people get lucky and win, while others lose. That is speculating. You throw your money out and hope more returns to you. These people often fail to do their homework; they choose companies' stocks that are either overvalued, high in debt, or poorly managed. In the real estate market, these kinds of speculators do not look at cash flow analysis and what the impacts would be if there were a downturn in the market. The investor, on the other hand, checks out the company, looks at the numbers, and sees if there is value in the company and if it warrants a purchase. The same is true in real estate. The numbers are essential. An investor counts the costs. As Luke 14:28–30 says, *"Suppose one of you wants to build a tower. Won't you first sit down and estimate the cost to see if you have enough money to complete it? For if you lay the foundation and are not able to finish it, everyone who sees it will ridicule you, saying, 'This person began to build and wasn't able to finish.'"* Count the costs and accumulate the facts. Study the numbers before you make a purchase or business decision. Also, remember to read your contracts. As Tom Waits once said, *"The big print giveth and the little print taketh away."*[43]

In light of the distinction between investing and speculating, I will discuss three areas of investments: stocks, real estate, and opening your own business.

Investing in Stocks

Beware: I know very little about stocks, but here is my best attempt to jumpstart you.

During the stock boom of the late 1990s, companies' stock prices soared. Many books were written on the subject, such as: *The Motley Fools Rule Breakers, Rule Makers: The Foolish Guide to Picking Stocks*.[19] Some claimed we were in a new economy governed by new economic rules. While it is true that many people made considerable sums of money, many others lost money when these companies tanked. To avoid losses as much as possible, I believe the best time to buy is when stocks are falling, not when they are rising. Money can often be made in adjusting or falling markets. Since I am not an expert in the stock market, I learned the important questions to ask before purchasing a stock. Here are things you need to know:

1. **Book Value:** In stocks, ask what the book value of a company is. What this essentially means is the value at which an asset is carried on the balance sheet.

2. **Current Ratio:** Current ratio is your current assets divided by current liabilities of the company. It shows a company's ability to pay its current obligations from current assets.

3. **Market Capitalization:** This is book value at which a corporation is determined by the stock price of its issued and outstanding common stock.

4. **PE Ratio:** This means price-to-earnings ratio. It gives investors an idea of how much they are paying for a company's earning power. The higher the PE ratio (price to earnings), the more you are paying

for the company's earnings. Typically, PE ratios range between 15 and 20.

5.   **Price to Book Value**: This helps to determine whether a stock is overvalued or undervalued.

6.   **Total Debt to Equity Ratio**: This ratio shows to what extent an owner's equity can cushion creditors' claims in the event of liquidation.

I once posed these considerations to a financial advisor. He didn't know how to respond to these and told me that he just received his stock recommendations from his corporate office.

My opinion is that earnings should be the most important factor in choosing a company. Most of your publicly traded companies report their earnings four times per year. In the long run, profits are going to drive the price share. It does not always happen that way, but that's how it should happen. So if you can find a stockbroker that will help you work through these questions and give you satisfactory answers, go with him or her. If they cannot, find another stockbroker, or better, try to research these companies and figure this out yourself. Also, think long-term strategy. Scripture tells us to be cautious of hastiness (Prov. 21:5). Be like the tortoise who steadily plods along and eventually wins the race.

Real Estate

As I stated earlier, many have made a lot of money in real estate. At the same time, though, many have lost. We have seen a lot of speculators in this past market but few investors.

Unlike many other forms of investment, real estate investing is the easiest to find the numbers for. For example, if you are considering someday buying an apartment building or single-family residence, find out your capitalization rate and return on your investment. Study the neighborhoods, school districts, and locations for future growth in your area. Then take your annual rents minus your vacancy factor. You can find out the vacancy factor by comparing other rents in the neighborhood and researching the approximate vacancy factor of rentals in that area. Then factor in likely repairs, maintenance, broken windows, plumbing, painting, carpeting, and those types of things. Out of that, deduct your principal, interest, taxes, and insurance—the PITI. The remainder will be your monthly income—in other words, your net profit.

Now take your monthly net profit and multiply the figure times twelve. This is for the twelve months of a year. That will be your annual profit. Then divide your total profits by your down payment. That percentage is your rate of return. For example, let's say you made $10,000 this year. You would divide this back into your down payment, which was, say, $100,000. In this scenario, your return on investment (ROI) would be 10 percent. This does not include principal pay-down or depreciation of the property.

Some might say that when real estate is on a roll, it is difficult to get a property to cash flow. There is much truth in that. But here is the good news. As the real estate markets get tougher, you can obtain better yields because of the lower cost of purchasing the property. Often, rents will not fall as low as did the property value. So if rents remain close to the same, and property values drop, you will have a good chance to get a positive cash flow on your rental property. It is almost always better to get the cash flow now than to place all of your hope in the property appreciating in the future. Remember that if you generate cash flow now, then any appreciation will be icing on the cake.

> "A prudent man conceals knowledge, but the heart of fools proclaims folly."
> **Proverbs 12:23 (NASB)**

Before you make a purchase, however, there are things to be done. Run comparable sales of the neighborhood. Figure out what has been sold in that area over the past six months and compare those sales with the subject property. How does it stack up? Then, as you consider investing, study what the rents are in the neighborhood and see what kind of shape the building is in. If it is in poor shape, you might be able to clean up that property and increase the monthly rents. Ask the seller to show you their Schedule C form, which is their official expense sheet required for their 1040 tax returns. You can also ask for the last two years of bank statements for the property in order to see how much rent the property is actually collecting and how much the real expenses are. Many people, if asked how their property is performing, will not give accurate figures. Thus, this is a good way to check the real numbers of the property's performance. **The Bible tells us to be "wise as serpents and harmless doves"** (Matthew 10:16 KJV). The Schedule C and bank statements show all. They are the bottom line. If the people selling the property are honest, they should not mind releasing these things to you. But there are people who play games. It can be intimidating to ask for this, but it is necessary.

Another important factor in real estate—perhaps one of the most important, if possible—is to make your profit at the **beginning** of the purchase rather than at the end. In other words, buy low with your profit margin already built in. If things go wrong, at least you have built in some profit already. This is what investing is. Do not take a large negative cash flow when buying property. The Bible tells us to run this race of life unencumbered. But it is hard to support a family with the expenses of life in addition to a large negative cash flow. If you are fairly sure you can afford this and that there is an upside later, go ahead and take the risk. You can recoup if it becomes a problem. So count the cost. If everything checks out, go for it.

> "The plans of the diligent lead to profit."
> **Proverbs 21:5**

Do not be double-minded. I only wish I had been bolder and more trusting of God. I have gotten down to the point where I checked the numbers, knew it was a great deal, and then got cold feet. This is *double-mindedness*. That is where my little bit of insecurity has kept me from being all I can be. It is a lack of trust. If you have asked God to open and close the doors as He sees fit, and you have done everything legally, ethically, and morally, do not look back. And if you do make a mistake, realize that it is all part of the learning curve. So learn from it and be better for it.

Advice on Starting Your Own Business

If you wish to become an **entrepreneur**, you will need to consider many factors that play a part in opening a business. Factor in the terms of real money, time, strains on your family relationships, and the impact on your relationship with God. Learn to understand all of these factors before you take the leap.

I have heard it said that between **80 to 90 percent** of small businesses fail. There is a reason why: it is very difficult to open a company. So you must beat the odds. And the only way you can do this is by doing your homework.

Let me give you an example: there were two businesses right down the street from our home that I saw go out of business. The first made quiches. Although their business was on a busy corner, the product could not sell at the rate necessary to pay the expense of a prime location, the employees, and all of the other expenses of running a company. After only a year, this place went out of business. What if they had taken out a loan on their home to open this company? They would no longer have a company bringing in money but still would have a large payment for the loan. They are bound to the bank for years to come.

Right across the street from that business was a restaurant. The location it was in had been a restaurant five or six times, and each time the restaurant would go broke. Why would a third, fourth, fifth, and sixth potential owner come in knowing the owner before them had gone broke? I wondered why they would open a business there. I did not think it a good idea. And in the end, it, too, went out of business. The reason it went broke, I think, was that it was located on even a busier corner, where the average speed of cars passing by was probably about fifty miles per hour with no stop signs or stoplights. The traffic flow was moving too fast. As you came around the corner, you saw the restaurant, and by the time you thought about it, you would have already passed it. Yet, even after more failed businesses there, people continued to open up restaurants in this same location.

So, if you open a business, understand your key indicators, or KIs. Every business has its own KIs or measurements and benchmarks for that industry. Throughout my times as a businessman, I encountered a phrase that you only need to hear once for it to resonate forever: A knowledgeable CEO can run almost any business from a deserted island if and only if they possess that company's *key indicators* or KIs. KIs should paint a picture of how your business is doing.

Let me give you can example of some KIs that can help you understand and discern quickly how benchmarks work. For example, let us say that a mortgage company mails out approximately 20,000 advertisement pieces per month. On average, the response rate for this industry is 1.2 percent. This means if the company mails out 20,000 fliers per month, it should get approximately 240 inbound responses per month. This is one indicator. Now if that 1.2 percent drops, then this tells the company that it may have to redo its mailers, change the mailing list, or recognize that the market is getting tougher and increase mail-outs each month. Out of those 240 calls generated, the average conversion rate from "lead call to business partnership" has been approximately 32 percent. Now some loan officers are averaging over 40 percent while others are at 20 percent. So the results out of 240 calls is that the company gets an opening ratio of approximately 32 percent, which is about seventy-six loans per month. So if you have some loan officers at 20 percent, you need to either make them better with more training or replace them with better loan officers to raise that 32 percent to 38 percent, increasing sales.

The question you may be asking yourself at this point is this: why not just automatically increase that mailing list from 20,000 to 30,000 to 40,000 or perhaps 50,000 mailers per month to get more incoming calls? *The answer: the law of diminishing returns.* If a company is bringing an abundance of business clientele for its sales representatives, the more sales people tend to weed through the bunch in order to find the deals that will make the most money with as little work as possible. In short, they begin to cherry pick. Since there are plenty of leads coming in, they do not work the tough ones as thoroughly. If you do not believe me, here is another proof: the months of November and December are usually slower months. The leads are often cut in half. And every November and December, without fail, the inbound lead calls to loan ratio soars from 32 percent to nearly 45 percent. Fewer leads result in a higher conversion ratio. Why? With fewer leads, loan officers work them harder. In addition, they begin to go back to prior months and work old leads.

So what do these numbers say? Should I mail out more fliers? Not necessarily. Before I can even bring in more business, I would need to bring in more loan officers or improve the weaker ones, or both. So these KIs show a pattern in which our business is proceeding. All my KIs lead to one conclusion: **I must recruit.** Then I can increase my mailings and bring in more loans. I can also adjust my KIs for each loan officer to determine where they need help.

> *"Know well the condition of your flocks, and pay attention to your herds."*
> **Proverbs 27:23 (NASB)**

Understanding your KIs can make or break your business. In Luke 14, Jesus speaks of counting the costs. He says this in Luke 14:31, *"Or suppose a king is about to go to war against another king. Won't he first sit down and consider whether he is able with ten thousand men to oppose the one coming against him with 20,000?"*

So count the cost. Then you can conquer and put your neck on the line. This will save you much grief, and hopefully, you will reap more rewards.

Love,
Dad

Key Takeaways

1. Count the cost. Do your research.

2. Do not be hasty.

3. With a multitude of counselors, there is victory.

XIII.

THE CRITICAL IMPORTANCE OF GIVING

· · · · ·

"Examples are few of men ruined by giving." —Christian Bovee

Dear Children,

HOW DOES ONE expand his or her territory? Through generosity. In fact, the Word of God often teaches us things in a practical way, and giving is one of those things He asks. Though we have a duty apart from the benefits of obedience, it is true that God often blesses those who obey Him. Thus, there seem to be practical reasons for why we should tithe and how it benefits us.

Dr. Stephanie Boddie, of Washington University in St Louis, was quoted in a 2005 article on her university's website entitled, "Financial future may be brighter for those who tithe," summarizing a study by Boddie that was funded by the Annie E. Casey Foundation.[29] According to Boddie, *"People who donate money on a regular basis take a closer look at where their money is going. They are able to figure out and set aside the money they can donate on a weekly or monthly basis. This leads to more financial responsibility in the area of debt repayment and asset-building."* Boddie also said that tithing *"challenges attitudes and feelings towards God, finances, possessions, families, friends, the poor, the future and life in general."*

Rather than looking at tithing as a requirement, consider it a privilege. God is giving us an opportunity to succeed, for tithing teaches us valuable lessons. One such lesson is budgeting, for tithing requires that we carefully budget and pay close attention to bills, taxes, and savings. It teaches us responsibility and promotes personal discipline and thrift.

In addition, it is good that we thank the Lord that we have the opportunity and ability to give instead of depending upon others to give to us. We see how it benefits the less fortunate, feeds the hungry, and helps the community, the state, America, and the world.

Imagine if Christians didn't give. Most of America's hospitals and colleges would certainly not have been founded and would not be running today. We see millions of people who donate to colleges for scholarships. In many European nations, charitable and philanthropic causes that we take for granted in the United States are simply unavailable because people do not donate. As a consequence, there are fewer scholarships, youth programs, drug and alcohol recovery programs, or programs to help the disabled.

It becomes clear, by contrast, that America is a nation of givers. Americans are generous. In fact, the difference in giving between Americans and Europeans is not a difference of degree—it is a difference of kind. There are so many needs and areas to which we have to give our time, attention, and resources to be effective and make a change for the good. But those who choose to serve others are the foremost beneficiaries of service because it takes the focus off of self—and that's a good thing. This brings joy and purpose to a person's life. When we give, we learn to plan, watch, and carefully budget the money God has entrusted, and we tend to get better at it. We find more ways to stretch a dollar and more ways to save. Giving teaches good stewardship, which can lead to financial prosperity. Though it does not guarantee success, good stewardship is necessary to it.

For myself, I can say with confidence that, despite months in which we had been financially stretched, we have always managed to tithe. It has required us to watch the bottom line in order to ensure that enough is left over each month to give and pay our bills. It has encouraged frugality, and we have learned to invest prudently the money God has entrusted us. Also, our commitment to tithing has checked greediness in our hearts and has testified to our faith.

As I was studying the subject of tithing, I found over 245,000 articles on the subject. Titles of these include: "Baptist-to-Baptist Tithing," "Another Hindu Tithing," and even "Bingo and Tithing." I was amazed at how many articles were written on the subject, each with varying opinions. Even within Christian churches, I found great disparities in belief regarding tithing. Perhaps one of the best positions I found seemed to strike an appropriate balance. It comes from the mission of The Assembly of God, and though I'm not of this denomination, they state it rather well in their mission:

> *The Assembly of God denomination has always been a proponent of tithing ... We believe tithing is a recognition that everything we have comes from God ... The practice checks our greed, promotes personal discipline and thrift, testifies to our faith, promotes God's work in the world and alleviates human need ... While we do not believe tithing to be a condition for salvation, we do believe it is a very important biblical model, one which should set the minimal standard for Christian giving and more people of all income ranges.*[22]

It is a simple message and provides justification for tithing: God works through our generosity as we bless others and give back what is due Him.

Prior to marrying your mother, I heard a sermon on giving. The pastor talked about men inspired to give beyond the standard 10 percent. These men, he said, gave and continued to give as they grew in their faith. And each year, God continued to outgive them, and their businesses and bank accounts grew. Dr. Bill Bright, founder of Campus Crusade, used to be a businessman, and he found that the more he gave throughout his life, the more God expanded his territory in splendid ways. Norm Miller, CEO of Interstate Batteries, who first decided to serve God by giving everything back, saw a tremendous expansion of this business. There are other prominent men like Thomas Monahan, the billionaire founder of Domino's Pizza, whose experience was the same. Monahan gives and gives, and today, he is still a billionaire because God continuously outgives him. And we see the examples of the biblical models of Abraham, Jacob, and Moses, each of whom God blessed immensely.

It is important to remember that God understands our need to develop faith. And tithing is a means by which God's people will grow. If one can learn to trust God with money, then one can more ably trust Him in other areas of life. It seems tithing and faith are connected. In fact, tithing often reveals the maturity of the giver's faith. This is why 2 Corinthians 9:13 says: *"Because of the service by which you have proved yourselves, others will praise God for the obedience that accompanies your confession of the gospel of Christ, and for your generosity in sharing with them and with everyone else."*

> "I have observed 100,000 families over my years of investment counseling. I always saw greater prosperity with those families who tithe than those who didn't."
>
> **Sir John Templeton**

Please note, obedience accompanies their confession of the gospel. The way we give says much about the maturity of our faith and our commitment to true doctrine.

Over the years, I have had friends who found a million ways to justify their way out of tithing. These are well-meaning people, I am sure, but they are missing out on part of what it means to be a Christian when they claim that they are not obliged to tithe because they are *"not under the law*" (Rom. 6:15). Yet, years go by, and many of these people still struggle financially.

For example, one friend told me that, since he makes approximately thirty-five dollars an hour, he would donate a specific number of hours to the church each month instead of paying his monthly tithe. This, according to him, was his form of tithing. Yet this friend still struggles financially. He is only one example of the many who never learn the simple lessons of life: if you want to be great, serve; if you want to get more, give; if you want to be refreshed, refresh others. Proverbs 28:27 says, "*Those who gives to the poor will lack nothing.*" Likewise, Proverbs 11:24 states, "*One person gives freely, yet gains even more; another withholds unduly, but comes to poverty.*" Want more territory? Give some away.

Christ says this in Luke 16:10–11:

> *He who is faithful in a very little thing is faithful also in much; and he who is unrighteous in a very little thing is unrighteous also in much. Therefore if you have not been faithful in the use of righteous wealth, who will entrust the true riches to you? And if you have not been faithful in the use of that which is another's, who will give you that which is your own?*

So as the Nike commercial says, "*Just do it.*" Move past excuses into action. It will become easier to build your faith. Parting with one's money is difficult, but it is a good discipline. Francis Bacon said, "*Money is a great treasure that only increases as you give it away.*" It is a principle of the kingdom of God, which stands in resolute opposition to the standard wisdom of this world. While the world says, "*Get all you can and be self-serving,*" God calls us to give, for it is only then that we will gain.

> "A checkbook is a theological document. It will tell you who, and how, and what you worship."
> **Billy Graham**

Unfortunately, polling data indicates that most believers in America barely give at all. (And remember, this is in the most philanthropic nation in the Western world.) One estimate figures that the average Christian gives approximately 2.6 percent of his income away to charity, and only 8 to 11 percent of parishioners in any one congregation give on a regular basis.[37] This represents the lack of spiritual maturity among Christians and the view of money that suggests that it is theirs and not God's. And this view of money is often encouraged when we spend money on the wrong things, and worse, beyond our means. In doing so, we become saddled with debt and dig ourselves into an ever-deepening hole of financial obligation to others. It is when we are up to the hilt with debt and without money that tithing and being generous become even more elusive and difficult to do than they were before.

A popular discussion among Christians sounds much like the following: the commands contained in the Old Testament obliging us to tithe are no longer binding upon Christians, for tithing was a part of the old law under which we no longer live. Rather, we are now under grace.

This seems to me a true enough argument. The New Testament does not mention one word about tithing. However, it has much to say about giving. Paul writes in 2 Corinthians 9:7 that *"Each of you should give what you have decided in your heart to give, not reluctantly or under compulsion, for God loves a cheerful giver."* The point, then, is that we ought to give whatever we feel so long as we are cheerful. But we will get to that in a moment.

Let us first review what the Old Testament has to say to get a handle on the subject. I love the Old Testament, though many today seem to discount it. There are so many things in there for us to learn, especially from the mistakes and successes that the people who went before us made. On a theological level, it is hard to understand the New Testament without having a handle on the Old Testament. There are some things in the Old Testament that no longer apply to us—such as the dietary laws and the animal sacrifices—because Christ became the ultimate sacrifice. We also see in the Old

Testament that God communicated only with a few. In the New Testament, however, we see that the Holy Spirit communicates with all believers. In the Old Testament, salvation was offered to Israel; in the New Testament, God calls all men. Those are the basic differences. Other than that, the Old Testament is just as applicable as the New Testament. We still need the advice and wisdom of Proverbs and the comfort of Psalms. It is all timely today. Likewise, through Deuteronomy, Exodus, and Leviticus, among other books, we can learn from past mistakes of sinners like us.

By reading the Bible, we can learn about human nature, for the stories in it are essentially about us and our need for salvation. We make the same mistakes today.

From the very beginning of the book of Genesis, we can see Christ's footprints throughout the Old Testament and humanity's need for a savior. The law is also there to help us recognize what sin is and to recognize it in our own lives. The law is still holy, righteous, and good. As Paul says in Romans 7:7–14 (NASB):

What shall we say, then? Is the Law sin? May it never be! On the contrary, I would not have come to know sin except through the Law; for I would not have known about coveting if the Law had not said, 'You shall not covet.' But sin, taking opportunity through the commandment, produced in me coveting of every kind; for apart from the law sin is dead. I was once alive apart from the Law, but when the commandment came, sin became alive and I died; and this commandment, which was to result in life, proved to result in death for me; for sin, taking an opportunity through the commandment, deceived me and through it killed me. So then, the Law is holy, and the commandment is holy and righteous and good. Therefore, did that which is good become a cause of death for me? May it never be! Rather it was sin, in order that it might be shown to be sin by affecting my death through that which is good, so that through the commandment sin would be utterly sinful. For we know that the Law is spiritual, but I am of flesh, sold in bondage to sin.

Christ Himself said in Matthew 5:17, "*Do not think that I have come to abolish the Law or the Prophets; I have not come to abolish them but to fulfill them.*"

So where does this leave us? Well, the New Testament uses the word *giving*, whereas the Old Testament uses the word *tithing*. So what's the difference? Let's start in Deuteronomy 14:20–29; Leviticus 27:30 and 33 defines a tithe as the giving required by God of 10 percent of one's first fruits. Leviticus 19:9–10, Exodus 23:10–11, and Deuteronomy 26:12–15 indicate that there were additional forms of tithing. There was another 10 percent for national festivals. After that, there were still small tithes imposed to help the poor. In all, I estimate believers were required to pay approximately 25 percent of their first fruits (or gross income, as we would say today). What a commitment these people were required to make!

Then we have Malachi 8, a passage I have seen misused from the pulpit by pastors who attempt to guilt people into tithing. The text reads: "*Will a mere mortal rob God? Yet you rob me. But you ask, 'How are we robbing You?' 'In tithes and offerings.'*"

I once visited a church in Lake Havasu, Arizona, where the pastor used this Scripture and said, "If you don't give, you're robbing God, and robbers can't enter Heaven." He took great liberty in saying this, and in doing so, he distorted the meaning of it. I don't share his views, so I'll explain this verse in the proper context. But first, I would like to explain why some believers misuse the New Testament verse from 2 Corinthians 9:7, which states, "*Each of you should give what you have decided in your heart to give, not reluctantly or under compulsion, for God loves a cheerful giver.*"

Now Scripture in the New Testament doesn't say we have to tithe. It only says give. Many take this as an entitlement for themselves to decide how much. They then take it a step further and say that they are not supposed to give out of compulsion. True, the verse does say this, and I know this. But you, my children, I want to give you the best advice I can so that you will thrive. Essentially, what some say is that as long as you give and you can stay cheerful, that's all that is required because we're not under the law. And, of course, I do not advise that we do things under compulsion.

However, I must caution you. One can easily deceive themselves into thinking, "I can give whatever I want, as long as I do it cheerfully." But in this, remember that you are leaving a decision such as this up to a sinner who should, rather, throw caution to the wind. As a sinner, I can easily see myself starting at 10 percent of my income for tithing and then claiming that it does not make me cheerful. So then I decide upon 9 percent. Wait a minute. How about seven, six, five? Or, perhaps, even lower until I am cheerful at the national average of 2.6 percent.

But notice the context of the Corinthians passage: 2 Corinthians 9:6 says, "*Whoever sows sparingly will also reap sparingly, and whoever sows generously will also reap generously.*" Want to reap generously? Sow generously. Want to reap sparingly? Give sparingly. If you give 2.6 percent of your income, you are giving sparingly. Your harvest will be thin, and how can you stay cheerful with a small harvest? It is a simple principle of reaping and sowing. Now look at verse 7, which teaches, "*Each of you should give what you have decided in your heart to give, not reluctantly or under compulsion, for God loves a cheerful giver.*" Each person has purpose, and once you find it, you should not go back. God is faithful. Verse 8 says, "*And God is able to bless you abundantly, so that in all things at all times, having all that you need, you will abound in every good work.*" Then verse 10 says, "*Now he who supplies seed to the sower and bread for food will also supply and increase your store of seed and will enlarge the harvest of your righteousness.*" Verse 11: "*You will be enriched in every way so that you can be generous on every occasion, and through us your generosity will result in thanksgiving to God.*"

> "We make a living by what we get. We make a life by what we give."
> **Winston Churchill**

Instead of giving or tithing until you feel cheerful, I suggest you consider hitting it from this angle. By faith, start at 10 percent and tear away any reluctance you might have, and work on your cheerfulness. The end result will be the benefit of the great promises found in the rest of those verses.

Now let's go back and review the Old Testament verse, starting in Malachi 3:8, and explore the verse in its proper context. To do this, we'll have to start in verse 7 and end in verse 10:

> *"Ever since the time of your ancestors you have turned away from My decrees and have not kept them. Return to Me, and I will return to you," says the Lord Almighty. "But you ask, 'How are we to return?' Will a mere mortal rob God? Yet you rob Me. But you ask, 'How are we robbing You?' In tithes and offerings. You are under a curse—your whole nation—because you are robbing Me. Bring the whole tithe into the storehouse, that there may be food in My house. <u>Test Me in this</u>," says the Lord Almighty, "and see if I will not throw open the floodgates of Heaven and pour out so much blessing that there will not be room enough to store it"* (emphasis mine).

In verse 7, God declares to the Israelites that they have turned away from his laws and decrees. How? Because they have not been tithing. These people have fallen away. They are immature. How do we know this? We know this because we know that they have withheld their tithes and offerings. But God says, *"Return to Me."* How? By showing obedience. By bringing tithes and offerings. Then, in verse 8, God makes an accusation, stating that *"you rob Me."* How? Again, by not tithing. This is an indictment God makes against His people because they are disobedient to His Word.

Now in verse 8, God does seem angry as He makes this indictment? Then consider verse 9, as He continues the accusation by telling them they are cursed. This cannot be good. But in verse 10, the tone of the conversation begins to change as we see God challenging His people by telling them to bring their offerings into the storehouse. So, He says, *"Test Me in this."* In fact, this is the only place I've found in the Scriptures where God says, *"Test Me."* We should take advantage of this because God doesn't say any other place that we can test Him. Put Him to the test and see if He antes up as we give, and see if His claims are true. What an opportunity to test the God of this universe with His permission.

But then notice the closing verses. It seems He greatly desires His people obeying Him. Then God announces His title as *"the Lord Almighty."* He doesn't just say, "The Lord" or "Almighty." I believe He is making a point. Though angry, He proclaims that He is the Lord Almighty, meaning He is able to do anything. And *"see if I will not throw open the floodgates of Heaven and pour out so much blessing that there will not be room enough to store it."*

Malachi 3:6 tells us, *"I the Lord do not change."* He is the same today as He was yesterday, and He will be the same tomorrow. He is not someone who changes his mind. His character does not change.

> **"Good will come to those who are generous."**
> **Psalms 112:5**

How, then, does our territory begin to expand? By giving. We tithe, and God says He will throw open the floodgates of Heaven and pour out so much blessing that we will not have enough room for it. I have seen this again and again in a number of people's lives who have walked with God and have consistently tithed for ten, fifteen, twenty years, or more. It seems that once a person makes the commitment to tithe, they will often remain a tither.

So, when we obey and give generously, God is still able to bless His people. Why? Because He is Almighty, fully able to pour out blessings. It is through God that many people I have seen have expanded their territory.

Another option, then, is what God says to His people in Malachi 3:11. *"I will prevent pests from devouring your crops, and the vines in your fields will not drop their fruit before it is ripe."*

Since Mom and I have been tithing, we have bought cheap washers and dryers, cheap refrigerators and all sorts of appliances, and cheap automobiles over the years. One thing we have noticed is that our things seem to last longer than other people's do. Some of these things have worked for nearly twenty years, and we're fortunate they did not break down sooner. I believe this has been a blessing. I am not mechanical. I do not work on such machines. We just run them into the ground till they break, and it seems like we have been fortunate on those things. Some would say that's luck. I, however, think otherwise.

> "A generous person will prosper; whoever refreshes others will be refreshed."
> **Proverbs 11:25**

In closing, let me offer you a few practical steps in giving.

First, start at 10 percent of your gross. Perhaps one day, you will give beyond this and not out of compulsion. Remember, God still wants our hearts more than He wants our money. Both, however, are related. Where is our heart? Is it enthralled with money or with Him?

Second, remember that the practice of tithing helps us to budget carefully. It challenges those sinful desires within our hearts. Also, in tithing, do not look for loopholes. Be careful leaving your freedom in Christ in the hands of a sinner (myself and yourself).

Third, accept God's challenges. Test Him by giving to Him your tithes and offerings.

Lastly, learn to give cheerfully. While the Old Testament instructs us to give 25 percent, it is interesting that the New Testament is silent about a percentage. Rather, we are told to give cheerfully.

It has crossed my mind that God knew that one day we would have communist and socialist governments that would take everything away from people. People have wondered why Christianity has died out in Europe. My analysis is that as communism and socialism rose and taxes rose, Christian charity declined. The church indeed did decline because it lost its reason to give, and with that, it lost its spirit of charity.

So as you give, beware of a time when the government could tax incomes at 80 or 90 percent, and it's not far off. During Jimmy Carter's years, the highest tax rate was 70 percent—Ronald Reagan came along and lowered that top tax rate to 28 percent, helping to create 19 million jobs in the private sector and spurring a new wave of private generosity to charitable causes. Americans are charitable, at least when they are free to be charitable.

When I was in the California Senate, I spent a lot of time giving speeches to nonprofit organizations and getting to know their leaders. I found that about 85 percent of giving to nonprofits ended up going to help people, as opposed to employee salaries and administration. By contrast, welfare organizations run by the state government pay a much higher share of salaries and other compensation. As a consequence, I worry that they lack the incentive to actually end poverty because they would work themselves out of a nicely-paying job.

The bottom line: if we want to maintain a limited, constitutional government, we should preserve as much space and freedom as possible for cheerful giving.

Within whatever capacity you have to give, give cheerfully. And after that, don't sweat it. He owns all the cattle on a thousand hills. Wait and see what He does.

Proverbs 3:9 says, "*Honor the Lord with your wealth, with the first fruits of all your crops, then your barns will be filled to overflowing.*" Then relax. Give Him what is His. As Deuteronomy tells us in chapter 8, verse 18, "*But remember the Lord our God, for it is He who gives you the ability to produce wealth, and so confirms His covenant.*" As one pastor said, "*Earn as much as you can; save as much as you can; invest as much as you can; give as much as you can.*" Sound advice. So make money, but serve God.

> "A lot of people are willing to give God the credit but not too willing to give him the cash."
> **Author unknown**

God needs to be the Lord over all areas of our lives, particularly in the area of finances and giving. It may not always happen as you want it to, but blessings usually follow. After the first sermon I had heard years ago, I figured out my monthly debts, how much I made, and how much tithing would cost me. My debt payments and tithes would be greater than my income. This represented to me the impossibility of tithing. I was upside down. But, by faith, I did it anyway. And within three days, I unexpectedly received three checks I had not anticipated. These not only paid my bills but put a little extra spending money in my pocket. After that, I committed to tithing consistently and have not looked back to this day.

This is my advice to you. Why? Because your dad loves you. I want you to have great things. I want you to have prosperity. I want your territory to expand, but I also want you to have the right balance on finances. **Above all, I want you to serve God. I have never prayed that you would be intelligent or wealthy—only that you would be good and serve God. And here's the bonus: good things tend to come when you are pursuing God.**

Best wishes.

Love,
Dad

XIV.

LEADERSHIP, PURPOSE, & DESTINY

• • • • • •

Dear Children,

THERE HAVE BEEN thousands of books written on the subject of leadership. I will list a few of these titles: *Leadership Extraordinaire, Primal Leadership, Versatile Leadership, Resonant Leadership, The Courageous Leader, The 21 Rules of Leadership,* or *31 Rules,* or *81 Rules.* I even saw a book entitled *Leadership for Nurses.* And it is not just books out there; there are also television programs and websites devoted to the subject and magazine articles and training seminars describing the seven key ways to become a leader. Familiarizing yourself with these resources is a good and prudent thing to do. It is a way of seeking counsel. But the question must be asked: are we all meant to be leaders? Or should there be a greater market for learning how to be a good follower?

The answer to the first question is no. Not everyone is called to be a leader. You cannot have all generals and no privates. The world does not work this way. The leaders must be fewer than the followers. The reason is simple: leadership implies leading people. If everyone is a leader, then it so happens that no one is a leader. I am not saying that one cannot become a leader or that he cannot be a leader in a certain sphere of his life. But the point is that the modern works on leadership have failed to tell people the most important things about leadership—and followership.

Something to consider from 1 Timothy 6:10, *"For the love of money some people have wandered from the faith and pierced themselves with many griefs."* I point this out because the same can be said about the unhealthy desire for power or leadership. I've seen this in business and politics. For the love of money, power, or leadership, some have ruined their marriages, dismantled their reputation, and have gone astray, so be careful what you seek.

As one climbs higher on the ladder of life, the more responsibility one has and the more blows you take from the people around you. Human nature tends to take joy in seeing the chinks in another person's armor. Often, people want to point out how the big person stumbles. This is inherently a part of a leader's life: taking criticism. So if one cannot handle this, he would not likely enjoy leadership and is more than likely not a leader. As they say, *"If you can't stand the heat, get out of the kitchen."* Leadership is not all people think it is. It involves risks, serious responsibility, much criticism, and little praise. Leaders must manage people, not just in their professional life but also in their personal life, as they bring their personal issues to work. In business, there are so many factors an owner has to deal with: tax laws, governmental regulations, customer complaints, a bad economy, recessions, inflation, his own personal problems, hiring and firing people, and the list goes on. It gets ridiculous.

So why would a person do this to himself? Perhaps desire, greed, pride. Maybe it is God's will for some. But I am of the belief that few are built for this. It looks fun from the outside, but there are so many more parts of leadership that are not.

My advice is this: If you are built for leadership, go for it. But if you are not, do not. Leadership can often bring grief, cause tensions within us, stress, and bad health. God makes some people, as I stated earlier, to be leaders, but He also makes some to be followers. Consider 1 Corinthians 12:12–14:

Just as a body, though one, has many parts, but all its many parts form one body, so it is with Christ. For we were all baptized by one Spirit so as to form one body—whether Jews or Greeks, slave or free—and we were all given the one Spirit to drink. Even so the body is not made up of one part but many.

Verses 17–29 continue,

If the whole body were an eye, where would be the sense of hearing? If the whole body were an ear, where would the sense of smell be? But in fact, God has arranged the parts of the body, every one of them, just as He wanted them to be. If they were all one part where would the body be? As it is, there are many parts, but one body.

The eye cannot say to the hand, "I don't need you!" And the head cannot say to the feet, "I don't need you!" On the contrary, those parts of the body that seem to be weaker are indispensable, and the parts that we think are less honorable, we treat with special honor. And the parts that are unpresentable are treated with special modesty, while our presentable parts need no special treatment. But God has put the body together, giving greater honor to the parts that lacked it, so that there should be no division in the body, but that its parts should have equal concern for each other. If one part suffers, every part suffers with it; if one part is honored, every part rejoices with it.

Now you are part of the body of Christ, and each one of you is a part of it. And God has placed in the church first of all apostles, second prophets, third teachers, then miracles, then gifts of healing, of helping, of guidance, and of different kinds of tongues. Are all apostles? Are all prophets? Are all teachers?

Now this is talking within the context of the church, which is made up of different parts—some weak, some strong. But life is much like this.

God has created us all different with varying degrees of talent. God made some CPAs, some carpenters, some NFL quarterbacks, and some ballet dancers. Not everyone can be a teacher or administrator or business owner. Some are stronger than others. I advise you to read as many books on leadership and business as possible to prepare. But always remember that when you are in a position of leadership, you will not always get the glory as one would like. Instead, you get complaints, criticism, and all of the blame for failure.

So you must ask yourself, are you cut out for leadership? Are you built for it? One indicator is having the ability to get knocked down and get back up again—multiple times. Consider the career of Winston Churchill: he lost his bid for Parliament the first time he ran; the second time he ran, he won. He climbed the political hierarchy only to lose his position in World War I and take the blame for a failed naval campaign outside of Turkey. After this, he worked back up to the heights of the British government, only to be put out of power in his fifties. He got back up again and became the prime minister when his country most needed him. And despite all that he did for England and the free world, he was thrown out of power before the war even ended. He then fought back and became the prime minister again six years later. Do you see the pattern? Every time he got knocked down, he would get back up again and work hard to resume a position of leadership. This is the sign of true leadership.

But achieving leadership and gaining money and power are not things that we should pursue for their own sake. For it is when we achieve these things that the question of what we should do with them becomes ever more important.

> "The greatest mistake a man can make is to be afraid of making one".
> **Elbert Hubbard**

For what purpose should we put these things to use? In short, we should gain these things in order to do good with them. The poor need the rich to feed them, the weak need the powerful to protect them, and the purposeless need leaders to guide them. If you seek wealth and power and positions of leadership for reasons contrary to the principles of justice, mercy, and charity, you ought not to seek those things. You must ask questions like these: will you use your power to influence others to make our country better? Will you give money to help feed the hungry and clothe the poor? Will your leadership position and wealth be able to open doors? If you have a business, will you disciple your employees? Will you also have a strategy to make them better? Will you leave your children an inheritance? Will you open a side business to teach your children how to work, be responsible, how to budget, how to minister, how to tithe? Before you step into those positions, answer those questions. You have been given a sacred duty by God to help and watch over others. And these things—wealth, power, and leadership—are means to these things, not ends in themselves. And there is great responsibility attached to them. Work on leadership qualities, and allow God to open the proper doors.

These things, however, bring with them great temptations and opportunities for sin. Thus, we must always be on our guard against sin. Consider the story of the powerful and rich King David from the Bible. He had everything one could want, but he let his temptations overcome him and fell into serious problems. This is the story from 2 Samuel 11:1–6:

> In the spring, at the time when kings go off to war, David sent Joab out with the king's men and the whole Israeli army. And they destroyed the Amorites and besieged Rabbah. But David remained in Jerusalem. One evening, David got up from his bed and walked around on the roof of the palace. From the roof, he saw a woman bathing. The woman was beautiful and David sent someone to find out about her. The man said, "Isn't that Bathsheba, the wife of Uriah?" Then David sent messengers to get her. She came to him and he slept with her.... The woman conceived and sent word to David saying, "I am pregnant." So David sent this word to Joab, "Send me Uriah."

David then begins to scheme in order to get Uriah to sleep with his wife so that Uriah will think that it was he who got his wife pregnant. However, since this doesn't work, David tells his general, Joab, to send Uriah to the front lines in the next battle so he would be killed. David not only becomes an adulterer but a deceiver and now a murderer. How did all this happen? **He had money, leadership, power, and time.** While he should have been at battle with the other kings, he was messing around. He had too much time and opportunity to get into trouble. David's power contributed to his downward spiral. While his power and money and position gave him opportunities for great things, they also gave him opportunities for great evil. This is why all of these things require great virtue to guard against their abuse.

Let us not forget, however, that similar things happen today. Many men, as they get into their forties or fifties and after they have made a few bucks, become full of themselves and leave their wives and marry younger women who like them for their money. These men are reduced to old fools. They ultimately bring great pain into their lives. Just as David had everything he could have wanted, his sins brought great pain into his life. Just read the Psalms. He knew what pain was, and he knew what it was to have a dark soul. I would not want to exchange my life for his. Therefore, let God give in His timing, and then, when the season's right, you will be able to handle it. As 1 Peter 5:6 says, *"Humble yourselves, therefore, under the God's mighty hand, that He may lift you up in due time."* This doesn't mean you stop being ambitious for what is good. Do all you can, and in that effort, allow God to lift you up His way. I'll be proud of you regardless of the path you choose.

In my own life, God has moved me from places I needed to move on from, and He has brought me to the places I needed to be.

Sometimes, there were difficult circumstances with employers that I had worked with. Though unpleasant, they proved to be good learning experiences and God's way of moving me on to eventually opening my own business. Even better, I've maintained a good relationship with that former employer. This experience taught me lessons on how to be a positive influence and guide in the lives of my employees. I haven't always viewed my job from this perspective, but I do now. I have realized that this job went beyond a source of income. Part of my purpose in running this company was to help whoever came through our doors become better at their job. At sales meetings, we talked about the importance of honesty, wisdom, industry, charity, fortitude, and other virtues. I noticed that as we got better and improved these qualities, my employees not only treated our customers better, but they also became better people at the office and home. I give God the credit for this wonderful thing.

I have been extremely fortunate that God has given me a life with purpose, allowing me to serve in the California State Senate with over one million constituents. This has given me the opportunity to speak to thousands of people, making the case for a limited constitutional government, morality, and family. God has opened the doors for me to speak with over 12,000 pastors throughout the United States, men of influence. I never wanted to squander these opportunities, so I tried to choose my words carefully and asked God to guide my words.

It's important to work hard and with all your might and leave the rest for God. He will lead and guide you and will make your efforts a part of His plan. So the bottom line is to seek Him and His kingdom. You do this by asking for wisdom and the ability to discern right from wrong. Remember that God is the true source of all that is good. So ask Him. Consider the following passages:

"And I will do whatever you ask in My name, so that the Father may be glorified in the Son. You may ask Me for anything in My name, and I will do it." —John 14:13–14

"In that day you will no longer ask Me anything. Very truly I tell you, My Father will give you whatever you ask in My name."   —John 16:23

"Therefore I tell you, whatever you ask for in prayer, believe that you have received it, and it will be yours."   —Mark 11:24

"Pray without ceasing."   —1 Thessalonians 5:17 (KJV)

My point is this: God tells us to ask Him, rely upon Him, and offer up our needs and concerns to Him. We should respond to what He has told us. And if you don't get your way, it is because He truly knows what is best for us. He knows what good gifts to give His children and what things we ought not to have. This is why we ought to be always content and ever thankful for what we have been given.

Love,
Dad

"And the Lord's servant must not be quarrelsome but must be kind to everyone, able to teach, not resentful. Opponents must be gently instructed, in the hope that God will grant them repentance leading them to a knowledge of the truth."
2 Timothy 2:24–25

XV.

DEFENDING FREEDOM

· · · · · ·

"If we depart from the principles of our ancestors, neglect religion and its institutions, are not attentive to the instruction of our youth in religious and moral duty, as well as in human literature, indulge a spirit of innovation, are indifferent to the moral character of rulers, and yield to the temptations to luxury and dissoluteness of manners, which increasing wealth presents, we shall soon find ourselves unable to support the constitutions which have been the pride of our Nation, and the admiration of the world. But if we diligently attend to all these things, set our own hearts unto all the words of the divine law, and command our children to observe and do them, it will be our life, and we shall prolong our days in this good land. The mouth of the Lord hath spoken it."
Reverend Samuel Kendal, 1804

Dear Children,

WHEN I WAS growing up, I was taught that there are two things you shouldn't discuss in polite company: religion and politics. But a casual study of history shows that two common ways people oppress others is through those two institutions. Perhaps, then, those are the two most important subjects to talk about.

Some say that Christians shouldn't be involved in politics. Why then are so many of the key figures in Scripture involved in politics? *Moses was sent to establish a country. King David was the leader of his country. Joseph and Esther were sent to save the political establishments of their respective days. Nehemiah was called to protect Israel. And the prophets Samuel and Jeremiah were sent to warn the political leaders of their day. Apostle Paul used the political system to appeal his case all the way to the highest court in Rome.* In more recent times, German Pastor Dietrich Bonhoeffer believed that Christians should be where the flames were the hottest, which is why he left pastoring for politics during the Nazi regime.

Acts 9:15 says that we—God's people—are to bear Christ's name to kings.

What is our responsibility to our country? It is to defend freedom and truth.

Dr. Larry Arnn, the president of Hillsdale College, has declared that America has entered its third great crisis.[4] He has compared events of today to what was happening in 1860, prior to the American Civil War. Today, we face a historic turning point: whether we will maintain our government of freedom, or whether we will descend into despotism, ruled by force with an aggressive hostility toward people of faith and the free markets.

Consider the political ideologies that have come to influence affairs in our time. Saul Alinsky wrote the book *Rules for Radicals: A Practical Primer for Realistic Radicals*, which amounts to a manual on how to destroy America.[1] Alinsky's admirers include Barack Obama and Hillary Clinton.[36]

Saul Alinsky wanted to divide America. But Lincoln said that a house divided against itself cannot stand.

And we are talking about more than a minor divide. We are told in Scripture that we wrestle not against flesh and blood but against principalities and powers, against spiritual forces in high places.

As I write this, our education system is in steep decline, Afghanistan fell to our enemies after our long and costly investments in that country, law enforcement is being decimated, and crime is skyrocketing—murders in California are on the rise in 2023.

What are we to do during these challenging times? As the children of Israel were leaving Egypt after hundreds of years of captivity under the Egyptian pharaohs, Moses promised them that they would be given new homes, fresh streams of water, and the peace and safety to enjoy those material blessings. But there was a caveat. In those thirty-four chapters, Moses reminds the people of Israel more than fifty times that it is all predicated on them following God's moral laws, decrees, and commands. If they want life, they must follow those biblical principles. They ignored those principles at the peril of death.

In 1805, Congressman Fisher Ames declared in an essay titled "The Dangers of American Liberty" that *"all history lies open for our warning, open like a church-yard, all whose lessons are solemn, and chiseled for eternity in the hard stone, lessons that whisper, O! that they could thunder to republics, 'your passions and vices forbid you to be free.'"* Much is at stake in America.

There are three things we must do in times like these.

First, we must pray for mercy and ask for God's help. As Benjamin Franklin said at the Constitutional Convention of 1787, *"If a sparrow cannot fall to the ground without God's notice, neither can a nation rise without His assistance."* We need to pray for our families, and we need to pray for the church. Many churches no longer teach about immorality as they once did. Many have become what I call "user-friendly, seeker-sensitive" churches. In many ways, that is not good for any of us. We are being destroyed for our lack of knowledge of biblical principles. We must return to the Scriptures and to faith. That is the primary thing we must do.

Second, we must rebuff the rising tide of political correctness. Political correctness is nothing new—it was very much part of the landscape in Lincoln's day and Churchill's day. It comes about when the other side cannot win and know they lack the arguments to win. They seek to silence those of us who seek to defend truth and liberty, and they seek to blame us for the failings of society.

Rather than conceding to their demands for silence, we must speak out. Was Christ silent before the Pharisees? Was Lincoln silent with the slaveholders? Neither should we be silent. When we are silent, evil wins. Scripture tells us to expose darkness (Ephesians 5:11) and "**demolish arguments and every pretension that sets itself up against the knowledge of God**" (2 Corinthians 10:5). When we are silent, we embolden darkness.

Christ has called us to be salt and light. We must speak out and defend truth. God is for us and not against us, but we must be for Him, and we must rally our fellow citizens to do the same.

Third, as a practical matter, we must restore our founding documents to their rightful place in American political life. These documents are the basis for our limited, constitutional government. We have a lot of work to do on this front, but our country and families are worth the effort. The Declaration of Independence is the heart and soul of the American idea, and the Constitution is the formal charter of our experiment in self-government. The Declaration was a letter to the King of Great Britain, notifying him that the colonies were severing their ties with Britain and declaring their independence. Lincoln

> "Ministers of the Gospel have more important business to attend to than secular crises, but, of course, liberty is more than a merely secular matter."
> – Rev. John Witherspoon, May 17, 1776

said that the Constitution rested on the Declaration. Indeed, he wrote in an 1861 fragment, the Declaration was like an *"apple of gold"* framed in a *"picture of silver,"* which was the Constitution.

Many today claim that the Constitution is a "living document." That would mean that truth changes. They can reinterpret the Constitution to mean whatever they want it to mean. But if you read the first paragraph of the Declaration, with its reference to the **"Laws of Nature and of Nature's God,"** you cannot escape the reality of truth as the underlying basis of the American founding. This understanding of the "Laws of Nature" stretches from the Greek and Roman philosophers to the great writers of the Judeo-Christian tradition all the way through to thinkers like John Locke and then down to the framers of the American republic. The Laws of Nature lead us to truth. And to acknowledge "Nature's God" is to affirm that God had placed these truths in the moral law written in every human heart, written in Scriptures, and written in the Natural Law contained in all of history. The next section of the Declaration declares, *"We hold these truths to be self-evident . . ."* If this truly forms the foundation of the Constitution, there is no way that the Constitution is a "living document." It is based on self-evident truth. It is based on the idea that all are *"created equal and endowed by their Creator with certain inalienable rights."* These rights are endowed by the Creator,

> *"It is blasphemy to call tyrants and oppressors God's ministers when magistrates rob and ruin the public instead of being guardians of its peace and welfare, they immediately cease to be the ordinance and ministers of God and no more deserve that glorious character than common pirates and highwaymen."*
> **– Pastor Jonathan Mayhew, "A Discourse Concerning Unlimited Submission and Non-Resistance to the Higher Power," December 31, 1750.**

not by the government. These rights include *"life, liberty, and the pursuit of happiness."*

The Declaration goes on to list the abuses by the king of Britain: cutting off trade with other parts of the world, imposing taxes without consent, depriving Americans of the benefit of trial by jury, taking away our charters and abolishing our most valuable laws, and many other grievances.

The phrase in the Declaration that I appreciate the most is the closing paragraph. It says, *"For the support of this Declaration, with a firm reliance on the protection of Divine Providence, we mutually pledge to each other our lives, our fortunes, and our sacred honor."* Think about those words; these founding members pledged their very lives, fortunes, and sacred honor. We, too, may be called upon to make sacrifices for the country we love.

Our Constitution

Our Constitution was established to keep the government limited in size so that citizens' rights would not be violated.

Today, unfortunately, the government has overrun us. It has become a behemoth, infringing on almost every area of our public and private lives, taking our freedoms away. The government has long since gone beyond the original intentions of the founders.

Under **Article I, Section 8**, Congress was only empowered to do seventeen things—eight of them concerning national defense, six about commerce (having government secure the rights of citizens and businesses, not the government), and the remainder about territories. Anything else was government overreach. It was a limited, constitutional government.

Local and state governments could certainly take on other responsibilities, and this was the spirit in which we entrusted parents and local school boards to run our school system at the local level. However, they proved that a dispersed system of education was highly effective. Under this federalist approach to educating our children, America had the number-one school system in the world. Then, in the 1970s, under the Carter Administration, the federal government established a one-size-fits-all, behemoth Department of Education. They took away local control. America's standing in academic rankings has plummeted. As the government moves further away from the people, it does them a disservice.

The Ninth Amendment states, "*The enumeration of the Constitution of certain rights shall not be construed to deny or disparage others retained by the people.*" Sadly, many judges and others in government today have forgotten that *we the people* have rights that are not granted by the government, only protected by the government. The government cannot and should not take them away.

To reclaim our rights, we do not need to amend the Constitution. Rather, we need citizens to learn the principles of the Constitution and then demand that we abide by them. But today, there is a fierce assault on our liberties, as well as our Founding Fathers. It is a deliberate attempt to weaken our strength. That is why our Constitution was designed with checks and balances, which are quickly disappearing.

As you consider these great documents, you can understand why we became the freest and most prosperous nation in history because of the goodness of those who founded our Nation and their commitment to God. The greatness of our founders can be attributed to their mentors, many of whom were pastors, the moral leaders of their day, men like Pastor Abraham Keteltas, who believed it was a Christian's obligation to resist tyranny. He believed that this fight between Britain and the colonies was the cause of Heaven against Hell, as he put it, "*the kind parent of the universe against the prince of darkness and the destroyer of the human race*".[23]

Our heritage is both wonderful and noble. Because of the principles contained in our founding documents, it did lead to the abolition of slavery under the leadership of Abraham Lincoln, who finished "*the magnificent structure,*" to use a phrase from Frederick Douglass. We can be proud of our heritage, knowing that America has set more people in other nations free than any other nation in history.

Consider America's greatness. We were the first nation to have freedom of speech, freedom of press, and freedom of religion enshrined in a constitution. In other countries, subjects were required to endorse and follow the religion of the king. Today we have religious freedom. We can't take that for granted. Nor can we take for granted that we are governed by consent. The first part of the Declaration of Independence tells us that *"to secure these rights, governments are instituted among men, deriving their just powers from the consent of the governed."* This means that we, the people, are the consenting authority for self-government. We must remind the politicians that they are to work for us and not against us. They are to be our servants and not our masters.

Yet today, the government has become too big and powerful. It was never meant to be that way. It was meant to be a government of, by, and for the people. As Ronald Reagan said in his 1989 Farewell Address, *"'We the People' tell the government what to do; it doesn't tell us. 'We the People' are the driver; the government is the car. And we decide where it should go, and by what route, and how fast."*[33]

This is why it is crucial that we restore the principles contained in our Declaration and Constitution back to their rightful place in American political life. Samuel Adams said, *"If you love wealth better than liberty, and tranquility of servitude better than animating contests of freedom, go home from us in peace. We ask not your counsel or arms. Crouch down and lick the hands which feed you. May your chains set lightly upon you, and may your countrymen forget that ye were our countrymen."* Life is not just about money and homes, fame, and fortune. Often, it is about Heaven versus Hell. We have an important job to do.

As the Lord's Prayer says, *"Give us this day our daily bread . . . Thy will be done on Earth as it is in Heaven."* It will take great men and women to restore this Nation. The destiny of America lies in your hands. What a tremendous responsibility you have, and as your father, I want you to understand how grateful I am for the greatest country ever, founded on the greatest precepts ever. I believe you're up to the task of helping to restore this great country. I believe God is preparing each one of you for this great work. Go with God. I love you.

I close with this quote from Proverbs 29:2: *"When the righteous thrive, the people rejoice; when the wicked rule the people groan."* Amen.

Love,
Dad

Key Takeaways

1. *Pray.*

2. *Oppose political correctness.*

3. *Support the restoration of our founding principles of a limited government.*

4. *Defend freedom and truth.*

XVI.

OUR CIVIC RESPONSIBILITY TO FUTURE GENERATIONS

· · · · ·

Dear Children:

THE MASSACHUSETTS DECLARATION of Rights of 1780 contain these words: *"the happiness of a people and the good order and preservation of civil government, essentially depend upon piety, religion, and morality."* While, I don't have all the answers, I do have some strong opinions. America faces some serious challenges, and I would like to discuss those challenges today.

If you want to know about socialism, 1 Samuel 8 is an explanation of what socialism can do to a country. There are many things in Scripture that we can gloss over, but we must study them if we are to have a nation that is prosperous and free.

I am not a pessimist. I am hopeful that in the end, we will survive the challenges we face today. But I do believe America will face some rough seas ahead. I remember what Nehemiah said, that the walls were down in his day. It seems that almost every foundation is down or seriously fractured.

When I was growing up in the 1950s and 1960s, life was good. We could roam the streets in almost any town in America without the fear of being shot or robbed or being offered drugs. Families were secure, divorce was rare, and America's prosperity was growing. I wish my children and grandchildren could experience the same thing.

Today, our challenges include the economic challenge of almost **$30 trillion** in debt being passed on to the next generation and inflation exceeding 7 percent (especially when you consider the measurements no longer counted in the consumer price index like housing, oil, food, and utilities).[40] There has been an alarming assault on law enforcement. Our streets are less safe, and police officers are resigning by the thousands. As I record this, we witness the attack of Russia on Ukraine, and now there is talk of a possible Third World War, especially when you consider the rise of China and its threat to the United States. Also, we witness the growing death toll of innocent babies—an estimated 60 million lost to abortion—victims to the rejection of the principle that all life is created in the image of God. Everywhere we see moral chaos. Romans 1 speaks of this immorality and its consequences, which brings me back to the sentiment expressed by the writers of the Massachusetts Declaration of Rights: *"the happiness of a people and the good order and preservation of civil government, essentially depend upon piety, religion, and morality."*

Consider the example of Abraham Lincoln. In 1858, Lincoln ran for the US Senate against Stephen Douglas, hoping to end slavery. He lost that race, but in 1860, Lincoln ran for president. Many did not want Lincoln to run because they doubted that ending slavery was a good platform on which to run for president. But he won. The country then was a house divided. It was a small country compared to today, not even one-tenth of the population today. Many lives were lost in the war. It was the first time in America we had institutional orphanages. In the South, thousands of children lost parents and were sent to orphanages. It was a time of death and destruction, not just of life but of property. The American people were asking when this terrible war would be over. Unlike politicians today, Lincoln actually addressed their question and didn't mince words. In his

Second Inaugural Address, he told them the way it was. Speaking of the two sides in the Civil War, he said:

Both read the same Bible, and pray to the same God, and each invokes His aid against the other. It may seem strange that any men should dare to ask a just God's assistance in wringing their bread from the sweat of other men's faces, but let us judge not, that we be not judged. The prayers of both should not be answered. That of neither has been answered fully. The Almighty has His own purposes. "Woe unto the world because of offenses; for it must needs be that offenses come, but woe to that man by whom the offense cometh." If we shall suppose that American slavery is one of those offenses which, in the providence of God, must needs come, but which, having continued through His appointed time, He now wills to remove, and that He gives to both North and South this terrible war as the woe due to those by whom the offense came, shall we discern therein any departure from those divine attributes which the believers in a living God always ascribe to Him? Fondly do we hope, fervently do we pray, that this mighty scourge of war may speedily pass away. Yet, if God wills that it continues until all the wealth piled by the bondsman's two hundred and fifty years of unrequited toil shall be sunk, and until every drop of blood drawn with the lash shall be paid by another drawn with the sword, as was said three thousand years ago, so still it must be said "the judgments of the Lord are true and righteous altogether."

That was sobering to me when I read that. Lincoln believed that innocent blood cries out from the ground for life. I found it sobering not just because of the circumstances Lincoln was addressing more than 150 years ago, but even more so because of the circumstances we face in our own day.

- What is our culpability as Americans in an age of mass abortion of our unborn?

- What is our culpability as Christian believers?
- What if Lincoln was correct that the judgments of the Lord are true and righteous altogether?
- What if Lincoln was right that the innocent blood cries out from the ground for justice?

If he was right, there is much we should be concerned about today. We should be particularly concerned about the scourge of abortion.

Some churches on Sanctity of Life Sunday spend five or ten minutes on the topic of abortion, but this is an issue we should be sober about. Jeremiah 1:4–5 says, *"The Word of the Lord came to me saying, 'Before I formed you in the womb I knew you, before you were born I set you apart; I appointed you as a prophet to the nations.'"* God has a plan for each life, including the unborn. To deny that and take the life of an innocent baby is a great sin. Therefore, we should pray and lobby and work to stop this hideous taking of life created in God's image.

Next, I encourage you to give a serious reading of Romans 1 and consider the seriousness of Paul's tone regarding sexual immorality. Verses 18 through 32 say this:

The wrath of God is being revealed from Heaven against all the godlessness and wickedness of people, who suppress the truth by their wickedness, since what may be known about God is plain to them, because God has made it plain to them. For since the creation of the world God's invisible qualities—His eternal power and divine nature—have been clearly seen, being understood from what has been made, so that people are without excuse.

For although they knew God, they neither glorified Him as God nor gave thanks to Him, but their thinking became futile and their foolish hearts were darkened. Although they claimed to be wise, they became fools and exchanged the glory of the immortal God for images made to look like a mortal human being and birds and animals and reptiles.

Therefore God gave them over in the sinful desires of their hearts to sexual impurity for the degrading of their bodies with one another. They exchanged the truth about God for a lie, and worshiped and served created things rather than the Creator—who is forever praised. Amen.

Because of this, God gave them over to shameful lusts. Even their women exchanged natural sexual relations for unnatural ones. In the same way the men also abandoned natural relations with women and were inflamed with lust for one another. Men committed shameful acts with other men, and received in themselves the due penalty for their error.

Furthermore, just as they did not think it worthwhile to retain the knowledge of God, so God gave them over to a depraved mind, so that they do what ought not to be done. They have become filled with every kind of wickedness, evil, greed and depravity. They are full of envy, murder, strife, deceit and malice. They are gossips, slanderers, God-haters, insolent, arrogant and boastful; they invent ways of doing evil; they disobey their parents; they have no understanding, no fidelity, no love, no mercy. Although they know God's righteous decree that those who do such things deserve death, they not only continue to do these very things but also approve of those who practice them.

Consider what Paul is saying and then consider where our society is today. What is in store for such a society as ours?

The stakes are high, and the enemy is fierce. The battle is not against flesh and blood, but it is against principalities of darkness. The book of Deuteronomy records the story of the children of Israel finally leaving Egypt for the promised land after four centuries of captivity. They journeyed on the promise that they would be given homes, prosperity, fresh streams of water, olive trees, pomegranate trees, vineyards, and the peace and safety to enjoy all of these things. However, Moses warns the children of Israel over fifty times that they must be careful to follow God's moral laws if they were to enjoy the blessings of the promised land. If they went contrary to God's moral laws, the nation risked destruction.

In 1776, Pastor Samuel West delivered a sermon in Boston titled "On the Right to Rebel Against Governors," in which he said the following:

> It is our duty to endeavor always to promote the general good; to do to all as we would be willing to be done by were we in their circumstances; to do justly, to love mercy, and to walk humbly before God. These are some of the laws of nature which every man in the world is bound to observe, and which whoever violates exposes himself to the resentment of mankind, the lashes of his own conscience, and the judgment of Heaven. This plainly shows that the highest state of liberty subjects us to the law of nature and the government of God. The most perfect freedom consists in obeying the dictates of right reason, and submitting to natural law. When a man goes beyond or contrary to the law of nature and reason, he becomes the slave of base passions and vile lusts; he introduces confusion and disorder into society, and brings misery and destruction upon himself. This, therefore, cannot be called a state of freedom, but a state of the vilest slavery and the most dreadful bondage. The servants of sin and corruption are subjected to the worst kind of tyranny in the universe. Hence, we conclude that where licentiousness begins, liberty ends.

Today, I worry that we in America are doing much that is contrary to God's moral laws.

There are options for us as believers.

First, we can pray. Samuel Adams once said, "We shall never be abandoned by Heaven while we act worthy of its aid and protection." In 2 Chronicles 7, God speaks to the children of Israel, though I think the principle applies to all nations: "*If my people, which are called by My name, shall humble themselves, and pray, and seek My face, and turn from their wicked ways; then will I hear from Heaven, and will forgive their sin, and will heal their land*" (KJV). God wants to turn His wrath away and heal the nations. We would therefore be wise to return to the faith of our fathers.

We would do well to heed the words of a national day of fasting in 1863, signed by President Lincoln:

> *We have been the recipients of the choicest bounties of Heaven. We have been preserved, these many years, in peace and prosperity. We have grown in numbers, wealth and power, as no other nation has ever grown. But we have forgotten God. We have forgotten the gracious hand which preserved us in peace, and multiplied and enriched and strengthened us; and we have vainly imagined, in the deceitfulness of our hearts, that all these blessings were produced by some superior wisdom and virtue of our own. Intoxicated with unbroken success, we have become too self-sufficient to feel the necessity of redeeming and preserving grace, too proud to pray to the God that made us!*

We would be wise to pray the same prayer, ask for God's mercy on our land, and act upon our duty to hand our country on to our children. God, would You give us success in this broken world?

A second solution can be found in recovering our knowledge of God's Word. One reason we are in trouble is because many of our churches have become soft and even call themselves "seeker sensitive" or "culturally relevant," meaning that they stay away from anything controversial.

When I was working in sales, I often read books about selling. There is a lot that goes into being an effective salesperson, but one of the principles **I learned is that you have to overcome the objections right up front.** You have to deal with the tough subjects, the elephant in the room. We are failing to do that in many of our churches today. We settle for easy listening that tickles the ears over the truths of God's Word, which can truly be challenging to us. If we are going to win as a church and preserve an inheritance to our children's children, we have to deal with the tough subjects and take those on first. We need to encourage and admonish our pastors to rise to the occasion.

As citizens, we must speak up and defend the truths of Scripture, as well as the political principles contained in our founding documents, which limit the government's power. Faith and politics—the two things we supposedly shouldn't talk about—are the two activities in which we must be engaged in order to restore America.

Here is what history has taught me, some of the greatest statesmen earned their respective titles because they were willing to take on the most difficult issues of their time. Lincoln took on slavery, Churchill took on Hitler, and Elijah took on the 850 false prophets. We should learn the lesson that it is more important to fear God than man so we can stand for righteousness in these turbulent times.

We need to learn these things and teach them to others. When we are silent, evil wins. Christ has called us to be salt and light. He called us to expose darkness. We are called, in 2 Corinthians 10:5, to *"demolish arguments and every pretension that sets itself up against the knowledge of God"* and to *"take captive every thought to make it obedient to Christ."*

Fathers are called to leave an inheritance to their children's children. We want to restore and return America back to what she once was. I am convinced that God is for us, not against us, but we must be for Him, and we must remind our fellow citizens of that.

I think of Winston Churchill leading his country through fifty-seven consecutive nights of bombing during the London Blitz. He always kept the positive outlook that when we do the right thing, we will prevail. As he said in a June 16, 1941, radio broadcast upon receiving an honorary degree from an American institution of higher education:

When great causes are on the move in the world, stirring all men's souls, drawing them from their firesides, casting aside comfort, wealth, and the pursuit of happiness in response to impulses at once awe-striking and irresistible, we learn that we are spirits, not animals, and that something is going on in space and time, and beyond space and time, which, whether we like it or not, spells duty.[10]

In that same radio broadcast in which Churchill spoke of *"great causes on the move in the world,"* he reminded us of our responsibilities as free people. He continued:

*Our future and that of many generations is at stake. We are sure that the character of human society will be shaped by the resolves we take and the deeds we do. We need not bewail the fact that we have been called upon to face such solemn responsibilities. We may be proud, and even rejoice amid our tribulations, that we have been born at this cardinal time for so great an age and so splendid an opportunity of **service here below*** (emphasis mine).

All I can say to that is *Amen,* and *Lord, have mercy on us.*

Love,
Dad

KEY TAKEAWAYS

1. *We must consider our own culpability in the decline of moral foundations.*

2. *Pray, recover, and teach God's Word.*

3. *Boldly talk about the difficult subjects, chiefly faith and politics.*

XVII.

CONCLUSION: THE WHOLE DUTY OF MAN

· · · · · ·

Dear Children,

I HAVE BEEN trying to impart to you what I believe are the best practices for your life over these few pages. Let me conclude by summing up the most important point I can make regarding the subject of life. Solomon, in Ecclesiastes 1:13, writes, *"I applied my mind to study and to explore by wisdom all that is done under the Heavens."*

Yet Solomon says even learning is like chasing after the wind; there are endless subjects to discuss. And then Solomon talks about laughter and says that this, too, can be meaningless and foolish. And then he describes his life and some of the things he accomplished:

I undertook great projects: I built houses for myself and planted vineyards. I made gardens and parks and planted all kinds of fruit trees in them. I made reservoirs to water groves of flourishing trees. I bought male and female slaves and had other slaves who were born in my house. I also owned more herds and flocks than anyone in Jerusalem before me. I amassed silver and gold for myself and the treasure of kings and provinces. I acquired male and female singers, and a harem as well—the delights of a man's heart. I became greater by far than anyone in Jerusalem before me. . . . I denied myself nothing my eyes could see; I refused my heart no pleasure.

He had it all. He denied his eyes nothing. He refused his heart no pleasure, women, sex, power, or prestige. He was second to none. But then he says that it was *"a chasing after the wind."* It was all meaningless. Promotions, positions of leadership, ownership—they are all meaningless. He says that men often pursue things in vain: *"Vanity of vanities…vanity of vanities; all is vanity,"* says Ecclesiastes 1:2 (KJV). But then he begins to turn the subject and recognizes that God has ordered everything according to His purpose. He sums up the whole duty of man. And the answer is found in Ecclesiastes 12:9–14:

Not only was the Teacher wise, but he also imparted knowledge to the people. He pondered and searched out and set in order many proverbs. The Teacher searched to find just the right words, and what he wrote was upright and true.

The words of the wise are like goads, their collected sayings like firmly embedded nails—given by one shepherd. Be warned, my son, of anything in addition to them.

*Of making many books to which there is no end, and much study wearies the body. Not all has been heard; here is the conclusion of the matter: **Fear God and keep His commandments**, for this is the duty of all mankind. For God will bring every deed into judgment, including every hidden thing, whether it is good or evil* (emphasis mine).

So what does life come down to? It comes down to fearing God and keeping His commandments. That is it. Plain and simple. Fear God and keep His commandments. Only two things to remember. If I have taught anything, don't forget these. If you do this, all else falls into line.

I believe your future will be exciting, so look forward to what God has in store. He is for you to give you a future and hope. **Be positive. Be persistent. I love you.**

Love,
Dad

Salvation Prayer

Dear Lord Jesus,
Thank you for dying for me on the Cross.
I ask you to please forgive me for all of my sins
and come into my heart
and be my Savior and Lord.
Amen!

"But seek first his kingdom and his righteousness, and all these things will be given to you as well. Therefore do not worry about tomorrow, for tomorrow will worry about itself. Each day has enough trouble of its own."
Matthew 6:33–34

ABOUT MIKE MORRELL

MIKE MORRELL IS a husband, father, grandfather, lifelong Californian, and a follower of Jesus Christ. *The Road to Restoring the Family* is a collection of Mike's advice and reflections based on the truths of the Bible, the inherited wisdom of some of the world's greatest thinkers, and Mike's life experiences as a business owner, family man, and California State senator.

Mike graduated from Damien High School in La Verne and earned his Bachelor of Arts degree in business at the University of La Verne. Mike began his professional career in the title industry. After breaking company records twice, he began his own business in Upland, serving as president of Provident Home Loans and Provident Real Estate. He incorporated his business in 1989.

Over his decades as a business owner, Mike gained a deep understanding of the issues faced by residents and businesses in the Inland Empire. His decade of service in the California Assembly and Senate were informed by a basic philosophy: the government exists to serve the public, not to be served by it. The right to private property, the gift of free enterprise, and the government by consent are central tenets of our Nation and its continued prosperity.

Mike has served on the board of directors for the Building Industry Association and the Board of the Rancho Cucamonga YMCA and the

Advisory Board for the Gary Anderson School of Business at UC Riverside. He was also a key member of the Inland Empire Economic Partnership and the Legislative Committee for the Citrus Valley Association of Realtors. Mike was a cofounder of the Inland Empire Prayer Breakfast, contributed to Inland Empire leadership for the City of Hope, and acts on the Advisory Board to the Pacific Justice Institute. He is proud to support Hillsdale College through the Parents Association, as well as the Claremont Institute President's Club.

Mike served in the California State Legislature and served in the following committees:

- Housing
- Public Safety
- Transportation
- Labor
- Banking
- Energy
- Health
- Economic Development

Senator Morrell has been named Legislator of the Year by the following organizations: Military Officers Association of America, California Young Republican Federation, and We Tip. AmPac named him Faith and Business Community Leader of the Year, and the National Federation of Independent Business awarded Senator Morrell the "Guardian of Small Business Award."

Mike and his wife Joanie have been married for over four decades and have four adult children. Kristen is an alumna of the Claremont Graduate School, David is a graduate of Hillsdale College and Yale Law School, Matthew is a graduate of Hillsdale College, and Christopher has a career in the supermarket industry.

BIBLIOGRAPHY

[1]. Alinsky, Saul. *Rules for Radicals: A Practical Primer for Realistic Radicals.*
New York: Random House, Inc., 1972.

[2]. Aquinas, St. Thomas. *The Summa Theologica of St. Thomas
Aquinas: Prima Secunda.* Scotts Valley: CreateSpace Independent
Publishing, 2012.

[3]. Arnn, Larry P. *Liberty and Learning: The Evolution of American
Education.* Hillsdale, MI: Hillsdale College Press, 2004.

[4]. Arnn, Larry P. "The Three Crises of the American Republic."
Interview with Hugh Hewitt. *Hillsdale Dialogues,* Hillsdale College,
March 6, 2015. Transcript. https://blog.hillsdale.edu/dialogues/
the-first-crisis-of-the-american-founding.

[5]. Augustine. *The City of God against the Pagans.* Cambridge: Cambridge
University Press, 2002.

[6]. Austin Kyle. "Why Are So Many College Students
Rejecting Their Faith?" Collegians for Christ Campus
Ministry, May 10, 2021.https://www.cfccampusministry.com/
why-are-so-many-college-students-rejecting-their-faith.

[7]. Berkley, George. *See This Image Siris: A Chain of Philosophical Reflections
and Inquiries Concerning the Virtues of Tar War, and Divers Other Subjects
Connected Together and Arising One from Another (1747).* Whitefish:
Kessinger Publishing, LLC., 2010.

[8].   Brown, D. R., S. C. Ndubuisi, and L. E. Gary. "Religiosity and Psychological Distress Among Blacks." *Journal of Religion and Health* 29, no. 1 (March 1990). https://doi.org/10.1007/BF00987095.

[9].   Burke, Thomas Jr. "Understanding Man and Society" *Imprimis* 26, no. 2 (February 1997). https://imprimis.hillsdale.edu/understanding-man-and-society/.

[10]. Churchill, Winston. "The Old Lion." *America's National Churchill Museum.* June 16, 1941. https://www.nationalchurchillmuseum.org/the-old-lion-1941.html.

[11]. Covey, Stephen R. *The 7 Habits of Highly Effective People: Powerful Lessons in Personal Change.* New York: Free Press, 2004.

[12]. Covey, Stephen R. *The Wisdom and Teachings of Stephen R. Covey.* New York: Free Press, 2004.

[13]. Danko, William and Thomas Stanley. *The Millionaire Next Door: The Surprising Secrets of America's Wealth.* New York: Gallery Books, 1998.

[14]. De Nemours, Du Pont. *National Education in the United States of America.* Whitefish: Literary Licensing, LLC., 2012.

[15]. Encounters with Religion. "University of Redlands confers honorary doctorate on HH Karmapa." Accessed March 25, 2015. https://begegnungenmitreligionen.wordpress.com/tag/buddhismus/page/3/.

[16]. Fagan, Patrick F., and Robert Rector. "The Effects of Divorce on America." *The Heritage Foundation* (June 2000). https://www.heritage.org/marriage-and-family/report/the-effects-divorce-america.

[17]. Family Law Act, 1969 Stats., ch. 1608, § 37 (1970).

[18]. Flannery, Christopher. "Educating Citizens–December, 1 2004". *Ashbrook Center,* edited by Larry P. Arnn, and Jeffrey, Douglas A. Ashland: The Claremont Institute, 1993.

[19]. Gardner, David, and Tom Gardner. *The Motley Fool's Rule Breakers, Rule Makers: The Foolish Guide to Picking Shares.* London: BoxTree, 2000.

[20]. Graham, Benjamin, and Jason Zweig. *The Intelligent Investor.* New York: HarperBusiness Essentials, 2006.

[21]. Hanson, Melanie. "Student Loan Debt Statistics." February 10, 2023. https://educationdata.org/student-loan-debt-statistics.

[22]. Hillsdale Assembly of God. "Giving." Accessed February 21, 2023. https://www.hillsdaleag.org/giving.html#:~:text=We%20believe%20 tithing%20is %20a,and%20helps%20alleviate%20human%20need.

[23]. Keteltas, Abraham. *God Arising and Pleading His People's Cause; or the American War...Shewn to be the Cause of God.* Newburyport: John Mycall for Edmund Sawyer, 1777.

[24]. Kinnaman, David. *Christians: More Like Jesus or Pharisees?* Barna Research Group. June 3, 2013. https://www.barna.com/research/ Christians-more-like-Jesus-or-pharisees/.

[25]. Lewis, C. S. *The Abolition of Man.* New York: HarperOne, 2015.

[26]. Lewis, C. S. *The Screwtape Letters.* New York: HarperOne, 2015.

[27]. A Man's Heart | Dr. Tony Evans at Promise Keepers Conference 2005. Accessed March 14, 2023. https://www.youtube.com/ watch?v=LErig9oGrpI.

[28]. Marshall, Ron. "How Many Ads Do You See in One Day?" *Red Crow Marketing.* September 5, 2015. https://www.redcrowmarketing. com/2015/09/10/many-ads-see-one-day/.

[29]. Martin, Jessica. "Financial Future may be Brighter for Those Who Tithe." *The Source, Washington University in St. Louis.* February 2, 2005. https://source.wustl.edu/2005/02/ financial-future-may-be-brighter-for-those-who-tithe/.

[30]. Matthews, D. A., M. E. McCullough, D. B. Larson, H. G. Koenig, J. P. Swyers, and M. G. Milano. "Religious Commitment and Health Status: a Review of the Research and Implications for Family Medicine." *Archives of Family Medicine* 7, no. 2 (March 1998). https://doi. org/10.1001/archfami.7.2.118.

[31]. Organisation for Economic Cooperation and Development Online Library (OECD). "Life expectancy at birth". 2021. https://doi.org/10.1787/27e0fc9d-en.

[32]. Pacific Coast Architecture Database. "University of Redlands, Memorial Chapel, Redlands, CA." Accessed December 19 2013. https://pcad.lib.washington.edu/building/18942/.

[33]. Reagan, Ronald. "Farewell Address to the Nation." *Ronald Reagan Presidential Library and Museum.* January 11 1989. https://www.reaganlibrary.gov/archives/speech/farewell-address-nation.

[34]. Reagan, Ronald, Kiron K. Skinner, Annelise Graebner Anderson, and Martin Anderson. *Reagan: A Life in Letters.* London: Free Press, 2005.

[35]. Richards, M., R. Hardy, and M. Wadsworth. "The Effects of Divorce and Separation on Mental Health in a National UK Birth Cohort." *Psychological medicine* 27, no. 5 (September 1997). https://doi.org/10.1017/s003329179700559x.

[36]. Rodham, Hillary Clinton. "There Is Only the Fight: An Analysis of the Alinsky Model." 1969. Dissertation.

[37]. Singletary, Michelle. "To Tithe, Make it First Item in Budget". *Boston.com.* November 7, 2004. *https://rchive.boston.com/business/personalfinance/articles/2004/11/07/to_tithe_make_it_first_item_in_budget/.*

[38]. Thornburgh, Tristan. "We Remember: Jim Abbott's No-Hitter Against the Indians 20 Years Ago Today". September 4, 2013. https://bleacherreport.com/articles/1761748-we-remember-jim-abbotts-no-hitter-against-the-indians-20-years-ago-today.

[39]. U.S. Department of Education. "California Department of Education Agrees to Pay the United States up to $3.3 Million to Settle Whistle Blower Fraud Allegations." September 19, 2002. https://www2.ed.gov/about/offices/list/oig/invtreports/ca092002.html.

[40]. U.S. Treasury Fiscal Data. "What is the National Debt?" Accessed February 19, 2023. https://fiscaldata.treasury.gov/americas-finance-guide/national-debt/.

[41]. University of Redlands Tumblr. Accessed February 19, 2023. https://universityofredlands.tumblr.com/.

[42]. Wachholtz, Amy B., and Kenneth I. Pargament. "Is Spirituality a Critical Ingredient of Meditation? Comparing the Effects of Spiritual Meditation, Secular Meditation, and Relaxation on Spiritual, Psychological, Cardiac, and Pain Outcomes." *Journal of Behavioral Medicine* 28, no. 4 (August 2005). https://doi.org/10.1007/s10865-005-9008-5.

[43]. Waits, Tom. "Step Right Up. Asylum, 1976. Accessed March 14, 2023. https://www.youtube.com/watch?v=MtsOGoBD7x8.

[44]. West, Thomas G. *Vindicating the Founders: Race, Sex, Class, and Justice in the Origins of America.* Lanham: Rowman and Littlefield, 2000.

[45]. Zettersten, Rolf. *Dr. Dobson: Turning Hearts toward Home: The Life and Principles of America's Family Advocate.* Houston: Word Publishing Group, 1989.

CPSIA information can be obtained
at www.ICGtesting.com
Printed in the USA
BVHW092045130423
662306BV00003B/3